THE POLITICS OF INCLUSION

Preparing Education Majors
for Urban Realities

THEMES OF URBAN AND INNER-CITY EDUCATION
Series Editors:
Fred Yeo, Southeast Missouri State University
Barry Kanpol, Indiana University-Purdue University, Fort Wayne

THE POLITICS OF INCLUSION

Preparing Education Majors
for Urban Realities

edited by

Barry Kanpol

Indiana University-Purdue University
Fort Wayne

 HAMPTON PRESS, INC.
CRESSKILL, NEW JERSEY

Printed in the United States of America

Library of Congress Cataloging-in-Publication Data

The politics of inclusion : preparing education majors for urban realities / edited by Barry Kanpol.
    p. cm. -- (Themes of urban and inner-city education)
Includes bibliographical references and indexes.
ISBN 1-57273-463-9 -- ISBN 1-57273-464-7
    1. Inclusive education--United States. 2. Curriculum planning--United States.
3. Multicultural education--United States. 4. Education, Urban--United States.
I. Kanpol, Barry. II. Series.

LC1201.P65 2005
371.9'043--dc22   2005046072

Hampton Press, Inc.
23 Broadway
Cresskill, NJ 07626

Contents

SECTION TWO: EDUCATIONAL REFORM

INTRODUCTION

The Politics of Inclusion and the Inclusion of Politics

Working Within the "Confines" of Where We Are

Barry Kanpol

Indiana University-Purdue University Fort Wayne

It was February 1998 and I had just visited Saint Joseph's University. I interviewed for an Educational Foundations position as well as potential chair of the Education Department. In my short visit to Saint Josephs, I learned a little of the Jesuit traditions—the mission to care for others, service, outreach, academic rigor and social justice. Above all, I learned that as a Catholic university, the above values are premised on a deeply ingrained spiritual connection . . . one that I dare say, if held true to its core, would mean that dialogue about such issues as race, class, and gender must become absolutely paramount to meet the value components of the university's mission statement.

As I walked pointedly up and down the corridors of the Education Department, I saw open cubicles for offices, with phones ringing so loudly that most faculty situated in nearby cubicles could not hear themselves speak. I heard along the grapevine that the Education Department was not considered very highly within the university structure, and learned that there was no representative general education requirement course in the main undergraduate curriculum. Truth be told . . . I have seen, heard, and felt this story my whole academic life.

1

I was offered the job at Saint Joseph's University as chair of the department. Given the contradictions that were apparent during my visit—a university espousing social justice, yet an education department lacking basic resources and respect as one small example—and the acquisition of qualitative data about the university and its Education Department, I gratefully accepted the job with one initial starting point in mind. The driving question to me in the summer of 1998, as I started at my new place of employment, was this: Can a Jesuit university remain true to a politics of inclusion, despite the obvious contradictions that existed structurally within the University, particularly as it related to its Education Department?

Although these words may seem somewhat harsh to some who might read this from other parts of the University, if there is hope for a flourishing democracy, inclusion, and social justice, then we all must own up or perhaps "confess" to the internal contradictions. On the one level, from a macro-perspective, a politics of inclusion means the ability to see, evaluate, and interpret the university structure as possessing social and cultural injustices and various contradictions as mentioned earlier. On another level, a micro-perspective, the inclusion of politics would mean creating the value-laden spaces for issues such as race, class, and gender disparities to raise themselves as deeply embedded structural concerns to be dealt with, such as curricular and policy-related issues and concerns. Obviously, spaces of hope reside on the Saint Joseph's campus. A ripe Gender Studies Department and a faith—justice component in the general education requirements curriculum are examples that render the possibility for a politics of inclusion and an inclusion of politics that in their macro structural formation and their micro everyday configurations are prime to challenge contradictions.

Saint Joseph's University sits a few miles from downtown Philadelphia. We are also located on the cusp of the rich main line of Philadelphia. There are 212,000 urban students, approximately 300 urban schools, and many, many leaders who have a stake in the education of urban youth. Philadelphia, like many urban sites (Anyon, 1997; Kozol, 1991; Yeo, 1997), falls prey to the logic of social class stereotype, teacher burnout, high teacher turnover, rigid accountability, and standardization of curriculum. This story has been written time and again.

My first challenge to the Education department was to view inclusion from multiple dimensions—dialogue for a year or so and write about it, struggle over our own differences, own up to our theoretical and practical limitations and become a spokesdepartment for the university regarding inclusionary practices. Put differently, could we discuss what it would look like to "become" a part of the University's mission statement, despite what I would argue to be the structural inequities and contradictions that we perceived concerning our own department, within the university infrastructure?

One thing is certain. I came to realize that making sense of the confusion of politics and inclusion would include, fortunately, a clear alignment of the university with the Education Department on issues of social justice. The Education Department wants to be a part of a structural university commitment to a politics of inclusion through service to others as well as by assisting in the reforming of urban public schools. At the same time, the inclusion of politics into our everyday operations within the Education Department, such as in our curriculum reorganization, interrogation of diversity issues, creation and implementation of policies regarding inclusion and so forth, filter through the Education Department to the university and seriously begin to question issues of social justice that the university prides itself on. We proudly are part of those politics as well.

The following chapters are a collective departmental effort to delineate what this politics of inclusion on a more structural/macro level might look like and the inclusion of politics on more micro levels are as related to urban and other sites, particularly as we think of the preservice teachers we send out to student teach yearly, and as we place ourselves with the structure of the university as a whole. Moreover, as a department we understand that any written text is a political one, a statement of a social condition, a theoretical treatise of where we are presently with perhaps a budding vision as to where we can go to.

Not all who participated in our bi-weekly discussions are included here for one reason or another. Moreover, two of the authors have moved to another employment site, myself as well. But know too, that all authors in this text as well as those not in these texts are a part of the growth process that we as a department are undergoing.

With the above in mind, the book is divided into two sections: Curriculum Integration and Educational Reform. In the first section Jeanne Brady (chap. 1) convincingly argues that a politics of inclusion can be centered around what she describes as curriculum integration. Brady carefully delineates that this form of curriculum is best served for our students by viewing it through a postmodern lense. Understood this way, Brady connects curriculum integration to various macro theoretical trends—namely critical multiculturalism, as well as feminist and postcolonial readings. She argues that we can no longer view curriculum as static pieces, but, true to a more critically integrated curriculum understanding, must travel beyond sterile definitions of curriculum integration, to multiple and interweaving forms of curricula, both practical and theoretical, that make up a "politics of inclusion."

In chapter 2, Jim Lee, both courageously and in an academic honest fashion, tackles the very difficult task of looking theoretically and practically at a standards based curriculum through the lens of both constructivist and critical learning projects designed to enable student's voices, histories and experiences to flourish. Not a simple task. Citing examples of what Lee describes as a "democratic culture of quality curriculum," he forcefully argues that a curriculum of this sort can run through the contradictory spaces occupied by a standards model—if and only if the constructivist view of race, class, and gender issues are connected to curriculum as a politics of inclusion.

In chapter 3, Mary Applegate's focus carries the ideas of curriculum generated by Jim Lee into the areas of curriculum knowledge through literacy education as connected to the concept of *voice*, a term enunciated by criticalists over the last decade or so. Using the literacy term, *active learners*, Applegate cleverly connects voice to active learning by not losing focus on the relationship of literacy to context, literature, readers, and writers. Meaning, it is argued, can wholistically be understood when voice is used as an umbrella to connect the above elements. Using this theoretical framework, Applegate connects theory to the urban classroom with the arguments that a practical politics of inclusion is a "humane" issue—with literacy as a vehicle in which, given the student's particular voice, meaning can and should be constructed to the particular urban context.

In chapter 4, Lee once again forcefully argues a theoretical point: Any politics of inclusion necessarily involves incorporating an open-minded view of multicultural education. Lee presents various pervasive theoretical and practical trends in multicultural education today. Although Lee has more "critical" leanings, his eclectic understanding of how teachers must challenge their curriculum becomes central to a politics of inclusion that incorporates both an understanding of and a creative outlet for a curriculum that centers its attention on multicultural education.

I have, in chapter 5, attempted to practicalize what curriculum integration, voice, and democracy may look when theory links to practice in the form of a 3-week unit plan. Five of my former students combine to tie student voice to an inclusionary politics of the everyday lifeworld of multiple ethnicities. This is also an attempt by me, at least in part, to practically link many of the prior chapters to issues of curriculum inclusion.

In Section II, Educational Reform, Thomas McDuffie (chap. 6) takes on educational reform in mathematics education by delineating the tensions involved in such a movement. After taking the reader through the state of the art in mathematics reform, McDuffie carefully portrays this reform as not being "inclusive" enough, if, in fact, it is to live up to its egalitarian purposes. To some extent, McDuffie is able to answer a call made earlier by Saltman in his delineation of a "critical" mathematics. Clearly, McDuffie critiques mathematics education as being too European and male, and in dire need of incorporating a greater commitment and a more genuine approach to ethnic diversity. Cultural linkages are what McDuffie is arguing for as a politics of inclusion that has as its core very practical applications for preservice students.

Robert Palestini (chap. 7) makes clear his understanding of the theoretical differences that occupy the spaces of school choice critique. Palestini offers readers a uniquely eclectic and inclusive view of school choice that combines the best of a critical pedagogy with personal and subjective experiences that speak to helping youngsters in need in order to support the reestablishment of democratic ideals in our schools. In a provocative theoretical treatise, Palestini confronts what at times are inconsistent multiple theoretical positions by clearly articulating their contradictions. It is this level of inquiry that allows Palestini to take a position on schools choice. If closely read, Palestini's position is articulated as a politics that invites us to open theoretical and practical debate on incorporating school choice from within multiple and intersecting theoretical and practical paradigms.

In the final chapter, Donna Perone argues that inclusion and school safety is a political issue of large magnitude. Perone explains that school safety issues have not typically connected race, class, and gender concerns, and thus by definition are exclusionary in nature. Rather than connect safety to a theoretically conservative or liberal approach, what Perone defines as an "either–or" view, she elaborates on how a critical politics of safety must through public debate reach out to establish issues of a redefined image of safety and the community as well as of safety and democratic ideals.

CONCLUSIONS

Perhaps frustratingly, but surely more honestly, academic integrity lies within the acceptance of difference as a form of open dialogue. Not all authors in these chapters are or have been "on the same page theoretically." This is typically evident in the myriad of different positions authors take up. Yet, such is the beauty of challenging our postmodern condition that one can look at issues of theoretical and practical differences squarely in the face and commonly struggle for a more righteous form of inclusion that we can democratically as well as politically negotiate and live with and by. Without these theoretical differences, we would all become clones struggling with these owning differences, and constantly dialoging over their substance becomes the "stuff" of democratic possibility.[1] The task of galvanizing faculty has at times been gut wrenchingly difficult, but quite often a pure joy. It is these moments of moving dialectically between differences and commonalities that I find the most rewarding as a chair—one that I hope will keep me/us

---

[1]This struggle has become abundantly clear in these chapters as many of the authors view "their" fields from multiple theoretical positions—conservative, liberal, and critical to name a few. It is within these theoretical walls that this department is attempting to define itself within the institution.

deeply contemplating the terrain of social justice, particularly as connected to educational reform and our own stake in the institution within which we work.

REFERENCES

Anyon, J. (1997) *Ghetto schooling: A political economy of urban educational reform.* New York: Teachers College Press.

Kozol, J. (1991). *Savage inequalities,*New York: Crown.

Yeo, F. (1997). *Urban education, multiculturalism and teacher education.* New York: Garland.

I

CURRICULUM INTEGRATION

1

Curriculum Integration as a Pedagogy of Inclusion

Jeanne F. Brady

Saint Joseph's University

The rapid social and cultural changes that have taken place over the last three decades are immense and moving in unpredictable ways. Shifting patterns of immigration and demographics, increased numbers of single-parent households, a growing violation between wealth and poverty, media influences and representations, and advances in technology have stretched and reshaped the traditional landscape of American society into a postmodern terrain. In turn, these cultural and societal changes have dramatically effected and created the unstable and shifting enterprise of traditional educational theory and reform (Hargreaves, 1994; Slattery, 1995).

Public education that was designed and implemented in an industrial society and supported assimilation of citizens into a "common culture" is incongruous in today's postmodern society. When children are more ethnically and racially diverse than any other time in U.S. history and poverty continues to increase with no change in sight (Olson, 2000), educators cannot assume a business-as-usual attitude. The conditions of racism, sexism, poverty, and alienation, embedded in the lives of children that make up

9

many of the classrooms in which teachers work, need to be addressed. Therefore, as part of the responsibility of those who participate in the educational arena—teacher educators, school administrators, and classroom teachers—we must face up to the gross inequities that so many of our children confront everyday.

With regard to these pressing issues, it is vital that we commit to the serious work of educational reforms that are inclusive for all who live and work in our institutional arenas. To create inclusive educational environments that improve the lives of children and develop pedagogical practices that takes seriously the identities, histories, and cultural location of students and teachers is crucial and complex. How does inclusive praxis emerge in the context of a postmodern terrain that characterizes schooling in the United States today? For successful educational reform to be imagined, a critical democratic project that supports in-depth research and analysis of multifarious elements structured around inclusive theories and practices is required. But for this chapter, I limit my examination to a small but integral part of the project, that of curriculum integration as a pedagogy of inclusion.

In this chapter, I develop a pedagogy of inclusion conceptualized within an integrated curriculum theory that extends beyond the confines of linear discipline knowledge boundaries. This is a curriculum theory that embraces a politics of inclusion as a critical democratic project intended to situate teachers and students as active agents for change (Beane, 1997). To clarify what I mean by a politics of inclusion, I first call into question the present multicultural debate to expose how inequity permeates much of its framework. Grounded within a critical multiculturalism, I then examine the underlying theoretical premise that supports curriculum integration as a pedagogy of inclusion. Following this, I explore the roles that both students and teachers engage. Finally, I attempt to link a pedagogy of inclusion to a critical democratic project framed within a critical discourse of postmodernism.

THE MULTICULTURAL DEBATE

Theories of schooling have been disputed over many decades, and continue to remain complex and heated. More specifically, the present version of one of the debates takes place within the realm of multiculturalism (Darder, 1995; Kanpol, 1994; McLaren, 1997; Nieto, 1996; Sleeter & Grant, 1994; Taylor, 1994). This is no surprise as predictions maintain that members of minority groups in the United States will increase to more than 50% percent in our lifetime (Olson, 2000).

The varied and conflicting depictions of multiculturalism are important to differentiate because diversity is named as a significant remedy for much of what is viewed as unjust. However, in the name of diversity, contradictory policies and practices are put forth, which in some instances supports and in other instances, exploits and oppresses the many it affects. Although there are numerous distinctions made in the research on multiculturalism, for this section of the chapter I limit my overview of this debate to three general categories: conservative, liberal, and critical.

Multiculturalism poses a dilemma to the conservatives. Within the conservative position in schools, multiculturalism is developed around a view of pluralism that supports a common culture. This, of course, has its roots in the version of public education within the industrial society and supports assimilation of its citizens. Assuming that justice already exists within our democracy, named within a discourse of pluralism, the call for cultural difference and becomes associated with a threat to national identity, viewed as a disruptive and a dangerous force against a unified American society. Less apparent, however, are the many conservative intellectuals who define multiculturalism in ways that produce and legitimate a discourse of standards and efficiency. In both instances, multiculturalism is viewed as the enemy within and therefore the conservative position attempts, at all costs, to preserve the status quo and to restabilize American life within the regime of the dominant, hierarchical society (Brady, 1995).

A liberal position on multiculturalism is, for the most part, inclusive and respectful of diversity, yet reduces difference to equivalence. By stripping the core substance of difference and confining diversity to issues of sameness, a liberal position on multiculturalism erases the possibilities to further democratize our present educational institutions. Unfortunately, within the liberal principles of diversity, consensus on procedural rules regulate and control the majority of interests in society (Brady, 1995; J. Fraser, 1997; Mouffe, 1996).

In summation, to simply talk about multiculturalism as the representation of groups previously excluded is ultimately a minor alteration and does not serve to advance democracy. In this sense, the political philosophy of conservative and liberal discourses does not progress beyond a public morality and its ultimate goal is to regulate the basic cultural, economic, and social structure of society. Rather than expanding on the notion of democracy, these perspectives situate the logic of the economy, generated by the language of management, accountability, and efficiency, as the primary platform from which public education must serve its democratic function.

A critical multiculturalism pushes much further; it is within the gaps that recognition and acceptance of difference is embraced and the politics of inclusion emerges. The politics of inclusion challenges the notion that any one specific culture has a monopoly on virtues or insights. It also offers the opportunity for raising questions about how categories of race, class, gender, and ethnicity get formed within the margins and center of power. I turn to the work of contemporary feminists and critical theorists to explore more deeply what the politics of inclusion might imply.

Contemporary feminist and postcolonial critics (N. Fraser, 1997; hooks, 1989; Mohanty, 1990; Spivak, 1991) argue that individuals need to understand their ethnicity in terms of a politics of location, positionality, and inclusion. Accordingly, one has to be positioned within a place to understand how one's identity is constructed through history, politics, and culture. These recent advances of feminist and postcolonial theories have unmasked racism, sexism, and classism in contemporary thought and in doing so have effectively expanded the notion of difference and the politics of inclusion. This work has situated people of color, Third World women and men, and working-class women and men in particular histories. Locating and specifying race, class, gender, and other forms of difference, expose how racial and sexual imperialism embedded in American society attempts to either erase or white-wash histories and identities of those who have been relegated to the margins. As a result, these critics, by means of feminist and postcolonial traditions and collective memories, have made clear how White, dominant culture and experiences have been essentialized within the dominant discourse to speak for all, regardless of their differences.

We can use these traditions and a collective memories to advance the politics of inclusion as an educational, oppositional discourse, where educators are able to enrich and redirect visions toward emancipatory possibilities that have often been ignored by the master narratives that guide much of traditional educational theory and practice. Accordingly, it is hoped that students and teachers will engage in multicultural, inclusive pedagogies to critically explore, as a democratic project, the different and diverse experiences they face everyday.

POSTMODERN DISCOURSE AND INCLUSIVE PEDAGOGY

Public schools, linear classroom practices, and teacher education programs continue to rely on a discourse of order, certainty, and accountability that are defined within the limitations of a traditional, modernist paradigm. Yet, the divisions and boundaries that serve to rigidly define subject disciplines, traditional pedagogical practices, and the everyday work of educators and students are called into question when a critical multicultural inclusive pedagogy is employed. When used as a tool to recognize multicultural differences, explore contradictions, and challenge established knowledge beliefs, a postmodern oppositional discourse[1] holds the greatest potential for a deeper and more radical restructuring of educational theory and practice.

Postmodern thought offers a diverse body of cultural criticism as it accommodates a contextual discourse. Put another way, intrinsic in postmodern thought is a set of attitudes, perspectives, and discursive practices created to challenge and modify modern ideas that have proved to be too broad or too narrow in their definition (Elkin, 1995). For example, by challenging the modernist disciplinary boundaries in fields such as sociology, education, psychology, feminism, literary and media studies, geography and architecture, to name a few, postmodernism provides interdisciplinary access to a more complex interpretation of knowledge and ideas.

Thus, a postmodern oppositional discourse, specifically related to this chapter, is interrelated to the domain of educational reform and broadens this discussion in two ways. First, postmodernism offers a language of critique that allows us to view major flaws in traditional educational theory and practice. Second, postmodernism challenges traditional educational discourse and curriculum theory by encouraging multidisciplinary access across curriculum and disciplines. For example, postmodern discourse ruptures traditional curricular notions by reconstructing curriculum as a form of hypertext in which boundaries are crossed and ideas are interconnected in the development of a more complex reading of knowledge.

The postmodern perspective is directly linked to a politics of inclusion because it appropriately calls for an acknowledgment and celebration of otherness. Many postmodern educational theorist (Slattery, 1995; Stabile, 1995) embrace a politics of inclusion through a postmodern theoretical discourse by confronting a number of problematic modernist assumptions and existing social relations that discourage and even expunge the voices of the symbolically dispossessed. The challenge to and transformation of existing social relations generates new spaces for critical discourse and simultaneously destabilizes narrow and rigid educational programs. In turn, a postmodern perspective is capable of invoking and embracing broad changes in educational philosophies. Finally, a postmodern perspective assists educators with

---

[1]Postmodern theory does not require one to abandon the values of universalism and rationalism, but rather, views these values situated in a deconstructive relationship along side of them. It is important to understand that the modernist tools of thought are not forgone. Furthermore, the rejection of modernist ideals and value is not the dividing moment between modernism and postmodernism rather it is the confrontation between the two that addresses the authority and nature of reason. The critical relationship between modernism and postmodernism is dialectical and dialogical. Therefore, postmodernism should be used as a tool to provide the lens from which a critical discourse can be generated. See Jameson (1998), Giroux (1999), Yeatman (1994).

both a critical language and a practical understanding so as to create a pedagogy of inclusion.

CURRICULUM INTEGRATION AS A PEDAGOGY OF INCLUSION

Situated within traditional educational theory, the conception of what constitutes official (sacred) knowledge continues to be narrowly defined within a sphere of physical and material inequality. Similarly, most teacher education programs and classroom curriculums remain firmly established in traditional, discipline-bound theories of education that support content-based official knowledge as the foundation for curriculum development and distribution (Brady, 1995). Nevertheless, there has been a gradual movement in creating a new version of official knowledge that integrates the perspectives of various groups (Apple, 1993). Subsequently, official knowledge has been expanded within textbooks, curriculum, and the like, to include additional narratives of previously excluded voices. Yet, a more inclusive version of official knowledge is still caught among discourses, practices, and structures associated with dominant theories of education and curriculum that continue to reproduce knowledge within hierarchical relationships. Ultimately, what is left out of the official curriculum are the ethical and critical democratic components defined within a politics of inclusion.

The questions of how and why discipline-based content knowledge is taught and for whom it serves are typical inquires from a critical standpoint. Unfortunately, what is perceived and practiced in most classrooms is discipline-based content knowledge that, for the most part, continues to be constrained within the limited domain of modernistic structures and conservative multiculturalism. With the emphasis on national standards, objective-based education, and increased graduation requirements, most school districts presume there is only one pathway to success. Therefore, many teachers are forced to instruct specific discipline-based content knowledge within the boundary of a limited classroom time frame. What is often left out of contained discipline-based knowledge construction, whether it be historical knowledge, forms of popular culture, or knowledge relating to people's everyday lives, is the pursuit of exploring and understanding the overlaps and interconnections that exist beyond content knowledge and instruction.

In opposition to specific discipline-based content knowledge instruction, school curriculum should be defined in ways that call into question static and absolute knowledge transmitted from teacher to student. Furthermore, curriculum should transpire as a combination of not only knowledge but also social relations and values that represent both particular and inclusive ways of life. What this means is that student experience, culture, and history must be given an important position in analyzing knowledge, always identifying it as a part of the relationship between culture and power within a postmodern society.

Curriculum integration, as a pedagogy of inclusion, can create new forms of knowledge through the emphasis on breaking down established disciplines and (re)creating supra disciplinary knowledge. Labeled as a curriculum design theory, Beane (1997) defined curriculum integration as being "concerned with enhancing the possibilities for personal and social integration through the organization of the curriculum around significant problems and issues, collaboratively identified by educators and young people, without regard for subject area lines" (p. 19). At issue here is neither ignoring the boundaries of discipline-based content knowledge nor simply fusing different disciplines, but creating theoretical paradigms, questions, and knowledge that cannot be taken up and only answered within a policed boundary of an existing discipline. Organizing themes within this curriculum design theory are drawn from everyday life as it is being lived and experienced within the construct of students' own identities. In this sense, curriculum integration, as pedagogy of inclusion, urges us to rethink how we pursue intellectual inquiry and how it translates into practice both within and beyond the school structure.

Curriculum integration provides opportunities for possibilities that extend beyond limited curriculum content and classroom instruction that is only geared to learning basic skills, general standards, technical modes of instruction and canonical knowledge. This does not in any way diminish the importance of standards and academic rigor as a part of education reforms, nor does it negate the basic skills students need to be educationally successful. In other words, we must provide students with the necessary skills and critical perspectives that support the emergence of counternarratives required for actual participation for a democratic society in the midst of changing demographics. The combination of the two, both in words and deeds, unites knowledge integration with democratic vision.

In his book, Beane (1997) identified four major components of curriculum integration that include experience integration, social integration, knowledge integration, and curriculum design integration. The initial planning of the curriculum originates with a central theme generated among teachers and students and moves outward in a schematic web by shaping activities used to explore the central theme. The discipline boundaries are disregarded as questions give way to complex interwoven ideas and investigations within this theory of curriculum design integration.

I offer words of caution because curriculum integration should not be mistaken for thematic teaching that incorporates an interdisciplinary or a multidisciplinary approach (Fogarty, 1991; Jacobs, 1989). In an attempt to explore knowledge from an alternative perspective, some school districts embrace thematic teaching. In this sense, interdisciplinary or multidisciplinary approaches align subject matter to a theme to decide what each subject can contribute to the topic at hand. When critically exposed, this approach is no more than a slightly modified version of discipline-based content knowledge practices devoid of an investigation of how themes originate, why they are identified or the democratic projects they serve. The theory, design, and application of curriculum integration is far more complex than the prepackaged integrated curriculum units that are being applauded by some school districts or the thematic interdisciplinary practices that bring friendly subject matter together.

TEACHERS' ROLES IN CURRICULUM INTEGRATION

Teachers hold important roles as members of the collaborative team in the theory and practice of curriculum integration. Creating curriculum for and with children and adolescents begins with real-life problems and concerns generated through everyday lived experiences. This is a shift in traditional power relations within the role that many teachers feel most comfortable. The traditional academician role that teachers often play as bearers of specific discipline knowledge gives way to the role of a transformative intellectual as she or he moves from center to margin in the task of challenging views and speaking from multiple knowledge-based sites (Dohrer, 1999; Giroux, 1989).

For teachers to speak and listen outside the dominant discourse and, yet, from a position of acceptance, I turn to Spivak (1991). Spivak called for "[the] unlearning of one's privilege, so that, not only does one become able to listen to that other constituency, but one learns to speak in such a way that one will be taken seriously by that other constituency" (p. 42). By engaging in the process of unlearning privilege, teachers' roles shift. This alteration enables them to address and deepen the political and pedagogical aspects of curriculum integration. For this to take place, first they must challenge the exclusionary discourse of dominant knowledge by carefully scrutinizing the ligitmation of White, middle-class codes. This suggests becoming more self-critical and reflective regarding how identity and place come together within knowledge construction. By attempting to shift paradigms rather than appropriate dominant educational discourse and space, teachers can focus on developing strategies of communication and inclusion. In this instance, teacher roles become that of transformative intellectuals (Giroux, 1989) who recognize how school knowledge is produced, where it comes from, and how it serves the interests of some while oppressing some. Second, teachers should understand students' culture within their classroom so as to confirm students' experiences, which is at times contradictory and need to be challenged, and to legitimate all students as subjects in history.

Beane (1997) identified five important elements of shifting teacher roles within practicing curriculum integration:

1. Share curriculum and other decision making with young people.
2. Focus more on the concerns of young people than on predetermined "scope and sequence" content guides.
3. Take on questions to which they do not know the answers and, therefore, to learn along with students.
4. Take seriously meanings constructed by students.
5. To advocate for young peoples' rights to have this kind of curriculum (p. 67).

As practicing intellectuals, teachers from various disciplines work together. They explore their own identity as educators and facilitators, as well as discern the myriad curricular, instructional, social, and political issues connected to elementary, middle school, and high school education. Thus, official knowledge from the specific discipline is not abandoned or rejected but rearranged into the context of the project and taught through pedagogical activities. Teachers are fully aware of the need and their professional responsibility to bring certain kinds of knowledge and experience to students, including information dictated through the state and local district mandates. Nevertheless, these pedagogies encompass critical examination in the lives of teachers and holds teachers equally responsible for both official knowledge and popular culture knowledge as they are both open to inquiry because both are socially constructed.

One of many ways that teachers might include students participation in curriculum planning would be for the teachers to ask students to produce questions or disclose concerns. A theme will then be generated around these discussions. Theorizing and analyzing the theme and its influence on identity formation becomes a site of struggle over meaning and values.

An example of a theme generated by teachers and students might be an analysis of a form of media and its construction of values within it. Looking at print texts, film, television, music videos, advertisements, toys, fashion, can provide the opportunity to re-theorize the processes through which individuals form and understand their identities. Films, for example, should be seen as serious objects of analysis, recognizing that they function as "teaching machines" in the process of identity construction, which means more than including them in the school curricula; it also requires educators and students to bring questions to bear on their form and content. Furthermore, educators must take seriously the need to develop pedagogical practices that teach students how to use media as a mode of self-expression and social activism, providing them with the opportunity to (re)create new identities yet unimagined. Recent groundbreaking work that uses hypermedia and other computer technologies like e-mail, Web sites, and Web chatrooms as avenues to construct new spaces of resistance can offer opportunities for political action.

Curriculum integration is a complex, and at time, laborious pedagogy for teachers. It is important to note the possible tensions in the collaborative nature of integration. Yet, forms of critical resistance and intervention can provide the basis for raising questions and creating strategies that could foster the democratic project.

STUDENTS' ROLES IN CURRICULUM INTEGRATION

A plethora of curriculum research supports the need for knowledge and information to be made relevant for students so that it not only strengthens their intellectual development but also makes the connection between knowledge construction and production and their everyday lives. To make curriculum "real" to students it should comprise three components. First, to make curriculum relevant it must be pertinent to the lived experiences of the students; second, it should be crucial to the students' understanding of the world; and third, it should generate creative applications of the youths' ideas and inquiries (Beane, 1997; Beyer, 1996; Britzman, 1991; Giroux, 1997). Furthermore, important democratic principles and practices take place as the social contexts move beyond the boundaries of classrooms and schoolyards, and become sites to be explored. At hand is the task of educating students to locate themselves in their own histories and simultaneously establish the conditions for them to function as a part of a wider democratic culture. As a political project, the social integration component addresses real-life issues of unemployment, illiteracy, poverty, youth gangs, homeless families, violence against children, and the refusal to recognize the relationship among inequality, power and difference in our own "democracy" (West, 1993). This entails students to raise questions of justice and ethics in social culture and everyday life and take action to unmask ways they depend on their sometimes simple acceptance of popular culture's values by theorizing the relationship among pleasure, desire, and responsibility and among identity, socioeconomic representations, and spectatorship. In this sense, critical postmodern discourses through the knowledge integration component can emerge in the gaps created in moments of struggle, disruption, and rebellion.

Without any attempt to change the concept of what constitutes a critical democracy, schools and society will continue to reproduce existing structures of power absent of the politics of inclusion. Any attempt to change the cultural, political, and social aspects of the dominant society will be seen as an attack on democracy. Yet, curriculum integration is fundamental as a postmodern discourse for developing a broader notion of democratic struggle and social justice. It is this section of democratic visions to which I now turn.

DEMOCRATIC VISIONS

At the heart of curriculum integration that approaches teaching and learning from a postmodern, inclusive perspective, is a notion of education that embraces democracy. Ayers (1994) commented:

> The purpose of education in a democracy is to break down barriers, to overcome obstacles, to open doors and minds and possibilities. Education is empowering and enabling, it points to strength, to critical capacity, to thoughtfulness and expanding capabilities. It aims at something deeper and richer than accepting codes and conventions. Education is linked to freedom, to the ability to see, to alter, to understand, to reinvent, to know and to change the world as we find it. (p. 63)

The logic of democracy alone, however, does not guarantee individual freedom or the respect for individual rights. Nor does democracy promise community action and collective justice. Yet, embracing curriculum integration as it has been outlined in this chapter, as its own political project, is a solid beginning. By linking critical knowledge with cultural action, students and teachers become active participants in society by shaping economic, social, cultural, and subjective formations that constitute their lives. In this sense, the practice of curriculum integration as inclusive knowledge extends beyond the classroom walls and is situated and practiced in a (re)engagement with the world, presenting endless challenges to the imagination and ethical action.

Curriculum integration is a broad theory of curriculum design linked to freedom and change. Curriculum integration proposes a shift from the discourse of discipline-based knowledge as content bound to an altered discourse that firmly establishes an understanding of democracy and ethics as the centerpiece. It includes particular views about the purpose of schooling and the nature of learning. To understand the theory and process of how knowledge gets constructed, theorized, and applied curriculum integration attempts to work reason and difference together. Therefore, inherent in the theory and philosophy of curriculum design integration is education as a moral and political practice. It means we must develop a conception of this curriculum design theory that acknowledges the complexities of both the productions of identities, competencies, and desires, and the possibilities for a democratic agenda for learning within and beyond schools.

Embedded in a postmodern critical discourse that integrates politicized compassion and justice, an integrated curriculum provides a democratic vision that takes up the struggle against inequality in both the public and private. In this sense, an integrated curriculum focuses on economic and social structures and is taken up in personal experiences and in all social arenas. As a politics of inclusion, curriculum integration can be used to raise questions about the margins and center, especially around the categories of race, class, and gender. In doing so, it offers a new way of reading history and knowledge. In the truest sense, the practice of democracy becomes a national standard in educational reform.

CONCLUSION

To meet the demanding needs of our changing social world, we must develop new perspectives and ethical practices for our teacher education programs, school administrators, and classroom teachers that travel beyond the existing traditional discourses of educational reform. Curriculum integration offers an alternative pathway to educational success as a critical democratic process. Not only does this pedagogy take the responsibility for national standards and education requirements generated through state and federal mandates, it also encompasses a critical examination of our own lives and our understanding of the complex practices of government, media, and popular culture that influence and control our everyday experiences. It encourages the creation of sites of struggle in which complex images, canonical themes and stories, and supposedly commonsense versions of reality are disputed. As a supra-disciplinary practice it is context specific and is about the making and unmaking of these contexts.

In remembering the warnings of postmodernism as "a terrain to be contested," any kind of curriculum reform should continue to be reexamined. When a pedagogy of inclusion is evaluated, its theory and practice need always to be problematized rather than assumed. Although this curriculum reform may create opportunities for improving conditions for human existence, it may also deepen existing inequities and generates others. In this way, the criteria used to evaluate a pedagogy of inclusion "should be considered [to expose] whether the acceptance of fragmentation/diversity might be an equally efficacious approach to addressing injustices in education" (Fendler, 2000, p. 23). This evaluation includes the questioning of teacher, student, and knowledge authority within its specific context that seeks to effect acceptance, conformity, and obedience; a sense of personal agency and individual and group empowerment; resistance to institutionalized power;

the nonhomogenization of the experience of women, people of color, and other groups; and the exposure and challenge of gendered, racist, homophobic, and classist discourses.

In conclusion, grounded in a critical tradition and collective memories, curriculum integration as a pedagogy of inclusion challenges all of us to refuse simplistic and derogatory images as well as misleading privileged positions through a commitment to social responsibilities, ethical considerations, and collective action.

REFERENCES

Apple, M. (1993). *Official knowledge: Democratic education in the conservative age.* New York: Routledge.

Ayers, W. (1994, May). Can city schools be saved? *Educational Leadership*, pp. 60-63.

Beane, J. (1997). *Curriculum integration: Designing the core of democratic education.* New York: Teachers College Press.

Beyer, L. (Ed.). (1996). *Creating democratic classrooms: The struggle to integrate theory and practice.* New York: Teachers College Press.

Brady, J. (1995). *Schooling young children: A feminist pedagogy of liberatory learning.* Albany: State University of New York Press.

Britzman, D. (1991). *Practice makes practice: A critical study of learning to teach.* Albany: State University of New York Press.

Darder, A. (1995). *Culture and difference.* Westport, CT: Bergin & Garvey.

Dohrer, T. (1999). *Preparing teachers for curriculum integration.* Unpublished doctoral dissertation. Pennsylvania State University, University Park, PA.

Elkin, D. (1995, September). Schools and family in the postmodern world. *Phi Delta Kappan*, pp. 8-14.

Fendler, L. (2000, April). *Solidarity, inclusion, and fragmentation in critical curriculum theory: Where does power go?* Paper presented at American Educational Research Association, New Orleans, LA.

Fogarty, R. (1991). *The mindful school: How to integrate curricula.* Palatine, IL: Skylight Publishing.

Fraser, J. (1997). *Reading, writing, and justice: School reform as if democracy matters.* Albany: State University of New York Press.

Fraser, N. (1997). *Justice interruptus: Critical reflections on the "postsocial" condition.* New York: Routledge.

Giroux, H. (1989). *Teachers as intellectuals.* Granby, MA: Bergin and Garvey.

Giroux, H. (1997). *Pedagogy and the politics of hope: Theory, culture and schooling.* Boulder, CO: Westview Press.

Giroux, H. (1999). Border youth, difference and postmodern education. In M. Castells, R. Flecha, P. Freire, H. Giroux, D. Macedo, & P. Willis (Eds.), *Critical education in the new information age* (pp. 93-116). Lanham, MD: Rowman & Littlefield.

Hargreaves, A. (1994). *Changing teachers, changing times: Teachers' work and culture in a postmodern age*. New York: Teachers College Press.

hooks, b. (1989). *Talking back*. Boston: South End Press.

Jacobs, H. (Ed.). (1989). *Interdisciplinary curriculum: Design and implementation*. Alexandria, VA: Association for Supervision and Curriculum Development.

Jameson, F. (1998). *The cultural turn: Selected writings on the postmodern: 1983-1998*. New York: Verso.

Kanpol, B. (1994). *Critical pedagogy: An introduction*. Westport, CT: Bergin & Garvey.

McLaren, P. (1997). *Revolutionary multiculturalism: Pedagogy of dissent for the new millennium*. Boulder, CO: Westview Press.

Mohanty, C. (1990). On race and voice: Challenges for liberal education in the 1990's. *Cultural Critique, 14*.

Mouffe, C. (1996). Radical democracy and liberal democracy? In D. Trend (Ed.), *Radical democracy* (pp. 19-26). New York: Routledge.

Nieto, S. (1996). *Affirming diversity: The sociopolitical context of multicultural education*. White Plains, NY: Longman.

Olson, L. (2000). Children of change. *Education Week, 20*(4), 30-41.

Slattery, P. (1995). *Curriculum development in the postmodern era*. New York: Garland.

Sleeter, C., & Grant, C. (1994) *Making choices for multicultural education*. New York: Macmillan.

Spivak, G. (1991). Feminism and decolonialization. *Differences, 3*, 139-175.

Stabile, C. (1995). Postmodernism, feminism and Marx: Notes from the abyss. *Monthly Review, 47*, 89-107.

Taylor, C. (1994). The politics of recognition. In C. Taylor & A. Gutmann (Eds.), *Multiculturalism* (pp. 25-73). Princeton, NJ: Princeton University Press

West, C. (1993). *Race matters*. Boston: Beacon Press.

Yeatman, A. (1994) *Postmodern revisionings of the political*. New York: Routledge.

2

Constructivist Curriculum Standards

Resolving the Apparent Contradiction Through a Democratic Culture of Quality

James O. Lee
Saint Joseph's University

Cognitive science confirms Piaget's claim that learners construct their understanding of new learning by connecting it with personal experience (Resnick & Hall, 1998). Therefore, enacted school curriculums must merge with the voices and experiences of the students they serve if they are to be productive of substantive learning. But curriculums for the disenfranchised of our society, for those trapped in blighted urban schools serving the poor, often ignore the non-mainstream knowledge of the students they serve in favor of a curriculum designed by and for the dominant white culture (Yeo, 1997). Rather than a democratic curriculum of inclusion, minority students in the inner city usually receive one that excludes their experiences and voices. As Nieto (1995) explained, urban curriculums often proceed on the assumption that they must "tear down the building blocks the children already have in order to start from a middle-class foundation" (p. 38).

Instead of encouraging constructivist approaches to learning, the typical curriculum for the disenfranchised treats students as passive, empty vessels to be "filled up" with knowledge. Freire (1970) labeled this approach the *banking* concept of education, in which students are asked to receive, file, and store what educators assume they need to overcome perceived deficits (they are "empty" of what they need to succeed in life), rather than interacting with new learning on the basis of what they already know and can do.

Educators of the urban poor often believe they are addressing Kozol's (1991) "savage inequalities" by presenting the so-called "core" knowledge of the dominant culture, much as Hirsch (1997) recommended. That is, they believe that one way to provide for "equality" is for students to learn such knowledge, resulting in a more level "playing field," on which, to extend the metaphor, students can be more literate and compete more successfully for jobs.

After reviewing the associationist psychology that often informs the curriculum and instruction in schools serving minorities, this chapter analyzes constructivist pedagogy in conjunction with the current standards-based curriculum movement to determine if the marriage of constructivism with content standards is more supportive of democratic, inclusionary educational practices than is a deficit model of education.

Many of the national and local standards-based curriculums support this marriage. For example, in the "Overview" section of *Curriculum Frameworks*, the most recent curriculum of the School District of Philadelphia (1998), significant emphasis is given to constructivism as a "framework for organizing standards-driven teaching and learning." Also, many of the standards documents published by such professional organizations as the National Council of Teachers of Mathematics support student-centered pedagogy in which new learning is connected with current understandings and students' cognitive schemas.

But, although the use of the pedagogy of constructivism in support of content standards appears to offer hope for a more democratic education for minority students, I conclude that current approaches to implementing this marriage are at best very problematic and may, in fact, fail to better serve the learning potential of these students. I identify the reason for this failure as being rooted in the positivist tradition of assuming that knowledge—and therefore standards—has a life of its own apart from the learner's experience. Additionally, I explain how a liberal view of constructivism that ignores ethnic, class, and gender issues in favor of a more value neutral view of student experience is also responsible for this failure.[1]

---

[1]Kanpol (1995) maked the argument for an emancipatory, democratic constructivism based on critical and postmodern principles when he distinguished such a teaching and learning process from one that is liberal and progressive. For example, he contrasted the liberal view of constructivism as learning experiences connected to the learner's present knowledge and interests with a critical view based on experiences connected to the learner's knowledge about social conditions in relation to race, class, gender, and age.

Following this analysis, a project-based model of curriculum is presented that has greater potential for including the experiences and voices of the urban poor and that also effectively challenges them to meet standards of excellence. The apparent contradiction between constructivism and standards will be presented as resolvable with instruction that fosters a culture of quality through the use of learning projects that focus on a few important interdisciplinary standards. The concept of "constructivist standards" emerges as embodying the creative tensions of an oxymoron that can benefit both students and their teachers.

ASSOCIATIONIST PSYCHOLOGY IN URBAN SCHOOLS

Nieto (1995) referenced what Haberman (1991) labeled the *pedagogy of poverty*, which consists primarily of control techniques, including giving directions, making assignments, and monitoring seatwork. Textbooks, when they are available, are the dominant source of learning materials, and rote learning based on "skills and drills" is favored rather than creativity and critical thinking (Yeo, 1997). Such pedagogy emerges from what Resnick and Hall (1998) referred to as the associationist instructional theory that Thorndike and other psychologists promoted early in the 20th century on the basis of laboratory research that mainly involved animal learning. It has been largely discredited by modern cognitive science.

As Resnick and Hall explained, for associationists knowledge consists of a collection of bonds each of which involves a link between an external stimulus and an internal mental response. The goal of teaching is to strengthen the "good" or correct bonds and decrease the strength of the incorrect ones through a system of rewards and punishments, a process that echoes Skinnerian behaviorism. Resnick and Hall speak of the associationist's goal as one of "stamping in" the correct bonds and "stamping out" the incorrect ones.

This leads to a curriculum that focuses on the mastery of decontextualized, isolated bits of information and a pedagogy in which individual bonds are isolated for instruction.

Teaching based on associationist theory employs workbook drills for reinforcement, a form of recitation that has teachers asking a series of narrowly focused questions designed to trigger correct, factual responses with little forethought, and the use of tests that measure information items that are often unrelated. Teachers become mere managers of packaged programs and textbooks that require little intellectual engagement, and students are left with few strategies for creative thinking, problem solving, or the development of conceptual understandings. For example, students may memorize and be able to recite the Bill of Rights without making any connections to their own civil rights or civic and personal relationships.

Associationist teaching matches up well with a deficit model of urban education that believes students are cognitively, linguistically, and culturally in need of remediation that "stamps" in the dominate culture and "stamps" out the deficiencies that characterize a minority culture. Resnick and Hall's (1998) "stamping" metaphor connotes a curriculum that is imposed on minority students and that through high structure, repetition, and teaching in small incremental units can eventually replace deficiencies with the knowledge and skills of the dominant culture.

Such a curriculum fails to connect to the experiences that students bring to school, is mindlessly repetitive and therefore highly unmotivating, but is justified on the basis of a concept of "basic skills" that is reductionist and bereft of any rich intellectual content that might engage young minds. The logic of the old psychology is at work: One must "crawl before one can walk"; complex ideas and skills should be broken down into small, easy to learn component parts, especially for those with major deficits. Then the new learning from the dominant culture must be intensively drilled until it "takes," whereas the unwanted and undesirable behavior is removed or, to use a behavioral, stimulus–response term, *extinguished*.[2]

The influence of associationist psychology over the years has been pervasive and is largely responsible for educators failing to recognize that learning is culturally and socially constructed. As Alton-Lee, Nuthall, and Patrick explained (1993), the gender, class, and race of students influence how they negotiate their public and private participation in the enacted curriculum, and therefore the outcomes for students include not only what they learn from such a curriculum but what they learn about their own identity, value, and capability.

Alton-Lee et al. suggest four different ways that minority students may respond to the enacted curriculum. They may reject it as alien, distancing themselves from it. Or they may see it as something to be memorized or circumvented to avoid public humiliation. Alternatively, she may accommodate to it and be dismissive of her own experiences and perspectives. Or, finally,

---

[2]In fairness, it should be noted that there are linguists who believe that language learning contains both a system of rules network and an associationist network. For example, Steven Pinker believes that the irregular verb forms are memorized rather than produced by a rule-governing set of symbols. In summarizing Pinker's views in a review of his latest book, *Words and Rules*, Aronoff (1999) stated that Pinker thinks these two networks may actually reside in different parts of the brain. Such a possibility suggests that there can be a role for learning by association and that behavioral teaching strategies have their place in a teacher's repertoire of deliberative teaching methods.

they may feel relatively "at home" with it and even be empowered to evaluate and be critical of such knowledge. Although some minority students may be able to negotiate the dominant culture well enough to respond to it in a critical and empowering manner, the majority will respond in one or more of the first three ways, thereby either denying the value of their own culture and selfhood or effectively "dropping out" of the educational system.

CONSTRUCTIVIST PEDAGOGY

As noted at the outset, contemporary cognitive science confirms Piaget's claim that people construct their understanding of new knowledge and rejects the associationist theory of stamping in strong bonds between stimulus and response with repetitive drilling of isolated and decontextualized learning material. Learning is not a triggering of automatic responses; rather it is an interpretive and inferential process. Current mental schema are reshaped on the basis of new experience through an active reasoning that, for competent learners, becomes metacognitive—a conscious and deliberate reconceptualizing (or rethinking) of a concept or skill based on new information or new facility with its use.

Constructivism calls for a pedagogy that is student-centered, engaging learners actively in meaning-making activities that give form and shape to understandings and skills. It recognizes the potential of all learners to build their world of knowing and understanding through "meaning-full" learning experiences rich with possibilities for thinking and creating.

Because it is often the recommended pedagogy for standards-based curriculums, constructivist pedagogy is common in the popular educational press today. Many of the standards-based curriculums, such as Philadelphia's (1998) *Curriculum Frameworks* document, call for active student engagement in learning and the use of many different instructional strategies for helping all students succeed in meeting the standards. And because almost every state in the country has adopted content standards and are aligning them with standardized tests to measure student progress and provide for local accountability, constructivist pedagogy has taken on more importance in discussions of teaching and learning.

Zemelman, Daniels, and Hyde (1998) cited several characteristics of best practice recommendations in the various standards documents that reflect constructivist approaches to teaching. They summarized these "interlocking principles, assumptions, and theories" with the following descriptors: *student-centered, experiential, holistic, authentic, expressive, reflective, social, collaborative, democratic, cognitive, developmental*, and *challenging*. The picture these terms paint is one of students as reflective workers involved in meaningful learning projects the decisions about which are the students' responsibility, but with the support and input of the teacher and other students.

Implicit in such terms as *democratic, student-centered,* and *experiential* is the importance of the learner's cultural, social, and gender perspectives—a type of constructivism that is not value neutral. Unfortunately, these perspectives are often overlooked in urban schools, and teachers conclude that their students offer little on which to build a constructivist pedagogy.

STANDARDS-BASED CURRICULUMS

As previously noted, constructivist pedagogy is often recommended by national and local standards documents as an appropriate pedagogy for teaching content standards. The latter describe what it is that all students should know and be able to do; the emphasis is on what is learned rather than what is taught. Linked to content standards are performance standards that describe how good is good enough; they set the performance level for success and describe what students need to do to demonstrate their understanding or skill. Consistent with constructivism, performance standards descriptors usually focus on such learning processes as understanding, analyzing, comparing, creating, and problem solving, rather than on "mimetic" activities that merely call for repeating teacher or textbook formulations of ideas, a level of knowing that involves little if any active learning.

Most of the standards published by professional organizations and state departments of education have been developed by experts in a field, including university professors, professional scholars, and classroom teachers, who have identified that which constitutes essential knowledge and skills for all students. In many cases, these decisions are related to beliefs about the workplace abilities that students will need to be successful and to keep the country economically competitive in the 21st century. These include the ability to work collaboratively with many different kinds of people on real-world problems, to use the skills of analysis and critical thinking, to tackle issues that are many faceted, to be reflective in action, and to communicate successfully. They are presented as important abilities for all students, not just the top fifth of the student population that has traditionally excelled.

A curriculum based on content and performance standards and taught with a constructivist pedagogy appears to support a movement away from the sort and select, Industrial Age model of education to one in which all students experience a rich and challenging curriculum that is centered on what and how they learn. Thompson (1999), in an *Education Week* essay entitled "Confessions of a 'Standardisto'" reacted to Ohanian's (1999) anti-standards book, *One Size Fits Few,* by arguing that the standards-based movement is a break from the dominant factory model that has dominated 20th-century education. "The shift is from high expectations for some students to high expectations for all students; from a focus on coverage to a focus on results . . . from a focus on quantity to a focus on quality; from a focus on grades to a focus on student work" (p. 49). He believes that far from being an anti-democratic effort to standardize education for all students, as Ohanian maintained, standards-based programs can be tailored to the needs of individual schools, classrooms, and students, serving well the particular learning styles of students even while pursuing the same standards for all.

In the rhetoric of the standards movement, the emphasis is on "high" standards that, given enough time, adequate resources, and teacher training, all students are capable of achieving. The bell-shaped curve of grouping by ability gives way to a success for all philosophy that refuses to be content with the notion that only a relatively small percentage of students can succeed at high levels and that failure for some is inevitable. Such a belief in the learning potential of all students appears to be an appropriately positive, "can do" philosophy to take the place of the deficit model of teaching and learning that has characterized urban education. And it may seem especially appropriate when coupled with a constructivist pedagogy that stresses teaching major curriculum concepts in relation to students' experiences and prior knowledge, rather than in the context of the dominant culture.

CONSTRUCTIVIST STANDARDS: A CONTRADICTION IN TERMS?

A more thorough analysis of content and performance standards reveals problems. The overriding problem is that more often than not, the concept of "standards" reflects a belief that knowledge is, as Ohanian (1999) put it, "pure, and unrelated to the knowledge seeker" (p. 3)—in other words, not constructed by the learner and therefore not consistent with a constructivist view of learning. McDonald, Rogers, and Sizer (1993), in a Coalition of Essential Schools monograph, explained that much of the current work in creating standards reflects a liberal belief that "essential knowledge"—what all students should know and be able to do—can be identified, analyzed for its critical attributes, and assessed, and that therefore the standards that describe this knowledge are "relatively fixed and tangible things" (p. 2).

The great irony here is, of course, that this positivist view of knowledge runs counter to the constructivist pedagogy that many of the standard setting organizations are recommending! When standards are abstracted out of specific classroom settings by professional organizations and state departments of education and are deemed appropriate for all students, they often fail to connect to the lives of both teachers and their students. As Giroux

(1998) explained, knowledge "never speaks for itself, but rather is constantly mediated through the ideological and cultural experiences that students bring to the classroom" (p. 100).

The problem with viewing knowledge as existing apart from the experience of the learner can be illustrated with an example of a content standard that is common to social studies standards-based curriculums, although wording may vary: "All students will assess the likely causes of the Depression and analyze its effect on ordinary people in different parts of the nation." Although local educators may agree that this is an appropriate standard for their U.S. history course, a commitment to teach it involves visualizing its appropriateness in relation to the total learning experiences that different students will have in particular classrooms and in relation to other course considerations. As McDonald et al. explained "one cannot teach to a standard one is incapable of imagining" (p. 8).

Imagining in this case means that teachers must consider the importance of the standard in the universe of possibilities; they must determine how and where it might fit in their teaching, and they must decide what kind of student engagement with the standard would be appropriate given the competing demands of other course content, as well as the intellectual, social, and cultural contexts in which they teach and students learn. To what extent will students be ready to engage the standard in light of their previous learning and understandings? How will the cultural lives and experiences of urban students, the majority of whom are poor, connect to the experiences of those who suffered through the Depression? What sense will they be able to make of it? How do their lives compare with those who experienced the Depression? Will the study of the Depression promote a better understanding of how the students are connected across time and place with others who have suffered economically? Will the answers to these questions differ with different students? Different classrooms?

These are questions that invoke a constructivist perspective on learning. They get at the issue of the extent to which students and teachers are included or excluded in deciding on curriculum. Standards imposed on schools that are stripped of these considerations, or that do not allow for professional judgments about their appropriateness in light of such considerations, will undoubtedly be taught as knowledge to be received rather than to be constructed. These questions also expose the importance of viewing standards from a critical perspective in which their marriage with constructivism includes the ethnic, cultural, social, and gender experiences of urban students and are not, therefore, value free or neutral.

If the content standards are also tied to standardized tests the results of which are used to assess the effectiveness of a teacher or school, then the likelihood increases that they will be taught for the test as isolated knowledge and skills existing apart from the learner's experiences and intentions.

And, finally, if there are a great many standards to be taught, as is true of the standards documents of many states and professional organizations, the chance that any of them will be taught to a level of understanding and application (as is often called for by accompanying performance standards!) is further reduced.

In summary, when the same standards are imposed on all teachers and students in the name of a common core of essential learnings that a group of "experts" has identified, and when teachers are then held accountable for teaching all of them, the result is a curriculum of exclusion in the most fundamental sense because the individual learner and the contexts in which he or she lives and learns have been removed from the curriculum development process. The standards documents may very well speak to the importance of constructivist pedagogy, and learning activities may call for problem solving, application, and other "higher order" thinking and creating processes, but very little of this will occur in the classroom. The promise of a constructivist approach to curriculum standards will have been compromised, resulting in little more than yesterday's behavioral objectives, minimum competencies, or other positivist conceptions of teaching and learning.

For students in urban schools this outcome would be particularly harmful because many of the content and skills that comprise the standards emerge out of the dominant culture. A curriculum of inclusion requires a constructivist pedagogy wedded to standards that are shaped by teachers and their students. The recommendations of the subject matter experts can be consulted and may be found useful, but unless learning begins with the experiences and voices of the students in particular urban schools, then as Alton-Lee et al. (1993) explained, many students will reject the enacted curriculum, finding it alien to their experience, or may memorize it to avoid humiliation, or accommodate to it as best they can, and in the process be dismissive of the value of their own experience and culture.

RESOLVING THE CONTRADICTION: BEGINNING WITH A CULTURE OF QUALITY

The remainder of this chapter argues that the concept of constructivist standards need not be a contradiction in terms but instead is capable of engendering a culture of quality that begins with the student's own experiences and focuses on a few important interdisciplinary habits of mind important for successful learning. As is seen here, such a culture does exist in some successful urban schools.

A culture of quality requires that students be treated as intelligent and capable of doing challenging work. This means they are placed in demanding, long-term intellectual environments, which support an effort-based view of ability. Resnick and Hall (1998) stated that learning goals negotiated by teachers and students that assume aptitude is "mutable through effort and is developed by taking an active stance toward learning and mastery opportunities" support an "incremental theory of intelligence." Such intelligence is "a repertoire of skills continuously expandable through one's efforts" (p. 105). Effort and ability are positively related; greater effort creates more ability. This view of learning and ability is in sharp contrast to the deficit model. Instead, it supports a learner-centered constructivism.

How do students develop effort-based beliefs about intelligence so that they have confidence in their ability to learn by making incremental progress over time? They do so when "they are continuously pressed to raise questions and accept challenges, to find solutions that are not immediately apparent, to explain concepts, justify their reasoning, and seek information" (p. 107). Students become smart by being treated as if they already were. How different a view of learning than that provided by the associationist paradigm!

An effort-based, incremental concept of learning supports the creation of a culture of quality in which, through an inclusionary approach to curriculum design, standards emerge from the on-going intellectual work of students and teachers, rather than being imposed from outside agencies or the state. In an Annenberg Institute monograph, *A Culture of Quality* Berger (1996), a 6th-grade public school teacher argued for a project model of learning in which a student's daily work is part of a long-range, purposeful endeavor that results in work being judged against shared standards. As Berger explained, the longer process that projects involve "allows time for multiple drafts, rehearsals, or experimental trials" as well as a "serious critique of unfinished work" by teachers, other students, and the student herself (p. 25). Skills are taught in the context of the projects, rather than in isolation. Standards emerge as students and teachers consider the criteria by which completed projects may be judged as excellent.

Rejecting cookbook, step-by-step recipes of prescribed procedures, authentic projects require students to make choices, judgments, and decisions, and to apply personal style. Berger's specific example is an assignment in which each student prepares a guidebook to a different local building involving, among other activities, conducting interviews, researching local history, consulting city records, taking photographs, preparing illustrations, composing a book layout, deciding on the tone of the presentation—activities that give the student the latitude to draw on personal interest and strengths and to apply personal judgment and style. In this case, the teacher provides the assignment frame, but students have freedom to move within it, to capitalize on their intellectual and creative talents in completing an authentic learning activity.

Assignments such as these are part of a school culture that supports personal decision making, a supportive community of learners, and the democratic values of freedom and responsibility. Standards emerge naturally out of such a culture. Projects are not finished until they meet clearly defined criteria and exemplars that both students and teachers support because "that is the way things are done here." Reconceiving and reworking assignments until they are the student's best work is part of the routine of a culture of quality. Assessment criteria embrace a wide range of possibilities for a given project and need not reflect external, prescriptive, and simplistic definitions of excellence, emerging instead out of a consideration of the diverse forms that quality student work assumes in the local context.

When students engage in challenging and authentic learning activities in which purposeful intellectual work is connected to the real world of problem solving and creative projects, and in which a critically supportive audience responds to work in progress, student motivation, and a commitment to do well—to meet high standards—increase dramatically. The classroom becomes a workshop in which teachers are attentive to student work by reminding, encouraging, praising, modeling, clarifying, or explaining—in other words, by providing context-sensitive teaching at the appropriate times. Such teaching is in the service of high standards that are inclusionary by serving the interests and personal styles of individual students intent on their own meaning making. It is only when students care about their own work that they begin to care about meeting standards.

CREATING A CULTURE OF QUALITY IN URBAN SCHOOLS

This is the view of learning that is characteristic of the most successful urban schools. Central Park East Secondary School (CPESS) is perhaps the best known example of a successful urban secondary school that focuses on a few important "habits of mind" that support sustained intellectual effort, on projects and performances that involve students in such effort, and on performance standards for judging the worth of the results. In the case of CPESS, the habits of mind are the abilities to weigh and use evidence, to see and understand differing viewpoints, to see connections and relationships, to imagine alternatives, and to assess implications and effect (Darling-Hammond, 1997). In order to graduate from CPESS, students must complete a series of performance demonstrations of their understanding and skill that draw on their disciplinary knowledge as well as their ability to make interdisciplinary connections. The school sustains a culture of quality characterized by a knowledge-based constructivism. Darling-Hammond cited other examples of schools that organize curriculum according to the same principle of helping young people learn to use their minds well.

Supporting such a curriculum, and essential to its success, are school structures that provide for smaller classes and personalization (e.g., by grouping students into "houses"), family involvement, reduced student loads, and shared planning time for teachers. Although these factors are beyond the scope of this chapter, they are critical to the successful implementation of the curriculum and unfortunately are often missing in many schools.

The new Philadelphia curriculum, *Curriculum Frameworks*, referred to earlier, is based on "cross-cutting competencies" that serve as interdisciplinary connections and promote habits of mind in relation to the acquisition of knowledge and skills in six areas: multicultural competence, citizenship, communication, technology, problem solving, and school-to-career. Moreover, the curriculum urges that project-based instruction be used that will "blend authentic, real-world experiences with rigorous academic study" and is described with such terms as *contextual, constructivist* and *experiential. Academic rigor* is another term the Philadelphia curriculum applies to such projects when they challenge students to use knowledge and methods of inquiry that are central to the various disciplines and that support the development of higher order thinking skills and habits of mind, such as searching for evidence and assuming different perspectives.

This concept of rigor is in sharp contrast to that which is equated with "hard" or "difficult" or achievable by only the very "best" students—a non-inclusionary concept that quickly judges the poor and disadvantaged as capable of only modest academic achievement at best. Using "rigor" as Resnick and Hall (1998) would define it, the Philadelphia curriculum is calling for students to be placed in demanding long-term intellectual environments where the rigor is in holding students accountable for intelligent behavior of the kind described earlier. In this respect, it echoes Berger's and CPESS' commitment to a culture of quality, of which academic rigor is a hallmark.

Unfortunately, the Philadelphia effort to join both discipline-based and interdisciplinary standards with a constructivism pedagogy does not appear to be taking hold, due to a lack of sufficient professional development and the district's commitment to a single standardized assessment instrument for determining the effectiveness of teaching to the standards. Although the content of the Philadelphia standards are inclusionary by design and can be meaningfully connected to the lives of the urban youth they serve, in many schools they are either ignored or merely paid lip service. The standardized test drives instruction, and the pedagogy of project based, constructivist learning struggles to gain a foothold in a school culture that, despite the new curriculum, often conceptualizes learning in the *banking* terms of Freire's (1970) metaphor.

THE MISSISSIPPI FREEDOM SCHOOLS AS A MODEL OF A DEMOCRATIC CURRICULUM FOR THE DISENFRANCHISED

Most schools fail to place students in learning environments requiring them to work persistently at challenging tasks. As long as schools must teach to a great many discrete standards for each of the disciplines, teachers will be overwhelmed with the pressure to cover (rather than "uncover") material, and constructivist standards emerging out of a culture of quality will remain an elusive dream of those of us who advocate them.

Nevertheless, if a culture of quality, rather than a long list of standards, becomes the priority of a school and if that culture is based on a project approach to learning coupled with a commitment to mining the richness of the experiences of students, then progress can be made toward the development of an inclusionary curriculum. An example of how this can be accomplished can be found in the curriculum of the Mississippi Freedom Schools of the 1960s, which is described here.

Chilcoat and Ligon (1999), in "'Helping to Make Democracy a Living Reality': The Curriculum Conference of the Mississippi Freedom Schools," described the creation of the Freedom Schools in 1963–1964 and the curriculum developed for them. The purpose of the schools, which operated in the summer months, was to provide "progressive and radical educators with a practical example for implementing critical pedagogy in the day-today practices of public school" (p. 43). In fact, the curriculum designed for these schools provides some helpful guidelines for developing an inclusionary curriculum based on constructivist standards. One can see from the description of the curriculum that follows that it was not value free or positivistic in design; instead, it drew directly on the immediate and historical perspectives of the disenfranchised for whom it was designed.

The goal of the Freedom Schools was to empower students to address the injustices of the Mississippi society — to become forces for social change. It was decided at the outset that the curriculum would not be didactic but would allow for student participation and the expression of feelings, as well as flexible enough to allow teachers to "shape their own curriculum in light of their individual skills and interests, their students' interests, and the resources available in the particular community" (p. 51). Four groups worked on four different divisions of the curriculum: providing leadership training for the students; providing remedial instruction in the different subject areas; studying contemporary issues and problems; and providing nonacademic activities, including recreational, cultural, and fieldwork opportunities.

The first of these four divisions, leadership development, resulted in a curriculum guide for teaching African-American history in a manner that would provide the content for "a process of ethical discourse and inquiry to recover past events unknown to them" (p. 53). Additionally, a Citizenship Curriculum was developed that focused on certain core questions, such as "Why are we in freedom schools?" "What alternatives does the Freedom Movement offer us?" "What does the majority culture have that we want (and don't want)?" and "What do we have that we want to keep?" These questions were to serve as catalysts for inquiring into the students' own experiences and then for discussing ways in which the students could take action to bring about change in their communities.

The second division, dealing with remedial instruction in basic skills, was to be integrated with the other divisions of the curriculum, and focused primarily on students' experiences. Verbal activities stressed connections to their daily lives; reading and writing activities focused on using various genres to develop comprehension, critical thinking skills, and creative expression. Content included personal and practical issues, as well as liberation activities, such as publicizing mass meetings, canvassing techniques, and statistical breakdown charts.

The third division of the curriculum, dealing with contemporary issues, suggested the use of case studies prepared by the students and dealing with civil rights issues. The pedagogy was to be "built on cooperating experiences, problem solving, collective investigation leading to deliberation of the problem and social action" (p. 58). Suggested materials included pictures, tapes, songs, newspaper articles, plays, and movies to enrich the writing. Once again, students would be drawing on their own experiences and would, as much as possible, use the case studies as a means of understanding and solving current injustices in Mississippi.

The fourth division of the freedom schools curriculum, nonacademic activities, included forming a network of student leaders throughout the state, working on voter registration, student government and publications, and engaging in such creative activities as drama, talent shows, and creative writing.

Chilcoat and Ligon (1991) explained the main thrust of this curriculum as follows:

> The repressive teaching that had caused African American children to become submissive, dominated students was replaced by an emancipatory curriculum and progressive teaching methods designed to empower students to critically examine existing conditions, gain the knowledge and confidence to activate change, and prepare themselves to contribute creatively and positively to their communities. The curriculum, which was designed to relate directly to the situations and experiences of the students, was drawn from a variety of sources outside the standard textbooks. Topics were selected to promote in-depth study and develop significant insights as students mastered relevant information, related new information to what they already knew, and applied new insights to current problems. (p. 62)

Clearly, the Mississippi Freedom Schools' curriculum was both constructivist and inclusionary. Additionally, it echoes current critical theory in its emancipatory goal, whose achievement depended on equipping students with the skills necessary to critically understand social injustices and the means of providing leadership for bringing about change. The curriculum developers designed projects and other activities that in some cases took the form of written curriculum and guides, but the caveat was always for teachers to adapt the material to the needs of their students. Because it was connected to real-world issues that directly affected the students, the curriculum was authentic, providing the motivation that comes when students care about their work because they have a personal investment in it and see its relationship to their present and future lives. It is through this caring about learning that a culture of quality begins to take hold.

Although designed as a special summer program that was not a part of the regular school year, the Freedom Schools curriculum offers a model for critical theorists and practitioners who are intent on teaching in urban schools for social change. It also serves as a model for liberal theorists and practitioners who, although not necessarily embracing a radical approach to social change, do support an inquiry, project-based curriculum that begins with the students' own experiences, connects them with real-world issues, and, whenever possible, includes an experiential, community-based component.

Like the Freedom School curriculum, urban schools can design interdisciplinary projects that include such components as reading and writing about an important topic or issue, often based in the social or natural sciences; computer work that includes research and data analysis; and creative expressions of feelings related to the topic using such forms as dance, music, art, tapes, and poetry. Additionally, critical or "essential" questions can provide the focus for a project or thematic unit. Like those examples provided in the leadership division of the Freedom Schools curriculum, these questions are open ended in design and invite different points of view and ongoing study. They build on personal knowledge and experience and challenge students to demonstrate an understanding of the relationship between what they are learning and larger community and world issues (Jorgensen, 1994/1995).

Standards emerge naturally out of such projects as students and teachers consider what makes for quality work. Quality is often defined in relation to how successfully the project achieves an authentic purpose—that is, how convincing, pleasurable, enlightening, or informing the student's work is for those for whom it was intended, whether classmates, other students and friends, or the larger community. Criteria for quality work become a natural consideration for students and teachers because the success of the project depends on them.

GUIDELINES FOR URBAN SCHOOL LEADERS COMMITTED TO CREATING A DEMOCRATIC CULTURE OF QUALITY BASED ON CONSTRUCTIVIST STANDARDS

Like the Mississippi Freedom Schools and CPESS, school leaders must bring their staff and communities together to develop broadly conceived curriculum standards that describe the educational purposes or habits of mind for which students need particular knowledge and skills. These standards may be similar to those developed by CPESS or the "cross-cutting competencies" that provide the larger framework for the Philadelphia curriculum. They are supported by specific descriptors of student work that "anchor" levels of excellence for each standard and that are developmentally appropriate for different benchmark in the K–12 program—for example, at Grades 2, 4, 8, 10, and 12.

To use another example, a school or district may agree on the following five interdisciplinary habits of mind: "All students will be knowledgeable learners, effective communicators, productive thinkers, collaborative workers, and responsible and productive citizens." Descriptors for "knowledgeable learners" might include having an in-depth understanding of key concepts and knowing how to use various resources to find information regarding different topics. "Responsible and productive citizens" might include taking a stand with respect to a social issue important to the student and being able to defend that position with evidence.

Once standards and accompanying descriptors have been determined, student projects are designed at the benchmark grades that bring together all of the standards. Examples include the kinds of performance demonstrations of learnings required of all students at CPESS and the "Senior Project" that in some high schools provides a culminating learning experience involving all of the standards. A project might include research on a topic of some social or cultural significance, a written report on findings and conclusions, and an oral summary of the research in front of a panel of teachers, administrators, and community members, who then ask questions of the student about the issues raised by the research. Additionally, each student might be expected to work with a community mentor who has some expertise about the student's topic and who could assist the student in using the community as a resource for the project.

This example calls for students to be successful with the five curriculum standards just listed: They must develop a depth of knowledge regarding their topic; employ highly effective communication skills; think carefully and perceptively about the issues involved in their research; collaborate successfully with a community mentor; and support opinions and conclusions about the topic in a responsible manner. Of special importance is that each student is involved in a purposeful, sustained intellectual environment in which students are assumed to be intelligent, and in which effort exerted on challenging tasks creates ability that is shaped and strengthened over time.

Student work is assessed based on criteria related to the standards and the specifics of the project. In reference to this example, teachers and students wrestle with such questions as: What kinds of evidence serve as indicators of being knowledgeable in more than a rote or superficial manner—of understanding an idea really well? What is good writing and speaking, and how does it vary depending on genre, audience, and social, and cultural context? How can the application of different thinking strategies be evaluated? What are the criteria for determining if collaborative learning is taking place? What are the characteristics of a research report based on an important social or cultural issue in which the author is demonstrating responsible and productive citizenship? Answers to these questions support a developmental perspective that views the learning of skills on a continuum from naïve to sophisticated, from novice and apprentice levels to that of an expert.

Assessment criteria may be translated into assessment rubrics that in turn are based on actual student products and performances. The longer the project-based curriculum is in place, the richer and more varied the array of examples of excellence that emerge. As teachers and students across the grades and subject areas continue from year to year to focus on the criteria for excellence contained in the curriculum standards, the quality of teaching to these standards as well as the projects themselves keep improving. This forces the redefining of benchmark indicators in favor of higher standards. What was initially good enough no longer is.

In the example just given, school leaders need to make certain that examples of excellent written work are reproduced, shared, and celebrated with students and the community, and that examples of outstanding oral presentations and other exhibitions of learning are videotaped and made available for review. In this way, the standards for a culture of quality are defined through concrete examples and images, which support the development of mental models of what the school means by excellence. Over time, a school deliberately builds a culture of quality as students, teachers, administrators, parents, and other community members compare student work against their growing internalization of standards of excellence that are inclusive of the richness of the ethnic, social, and cultural lives of the students.

Although not all learning will be embedded in sustained projects, teachers can design units of study that contain a variety of options to engage students in ways that focus on the same curriculum standards. These units may be thematic and driven by open-ended and provocative "essential" questions that engage student interest and require critical thinking and making connections with the larger community. The work of Wiggins and McTighe (1998) in *Understanding by Design* can be especially helpful in the design of such units.

A project-centered curriculum need not ignore the practical realities of dealing with state standards. A majority of state content standards are process skills (procedural knowledge) and can be aggregated in learning projects that provide meaningful contexts and purposes for them. Other content standards that include highly specific declarative knowledge can be integrated into projects and units of study that support the district or school's global, interdisciplinary standards.

CONCLUSION

A democratic, inclusionary curriculum based on constructivist standards can be a reality in urban schools. Project-based curriculum design is one potentially powerful means of achieving this goal because it engages students in sustained intellectual work based on student experiences and interests. It assumes that effort in achieving standards is developmental, resulting in increased abilities and greater commitment to learning.

Whether based on a critical, social activist platform, such as that of the Mississippi Freedom Schools, or a liberal one that honors diversity but does not produce a curriculum primarily committed to social activism,[3] a project based curriculum that begins with the students' own experiences is liberating and empowering in intention: it frees the learner from the mind numbing, associationist learning of a deficit model of education. It recognizes the importance of building understanding and skill from the rich ethnic, social, and cultural contexts that comprise the student's world.

But such a curriculum requires giving priority to standards that describe critical learning processes or habits of mind rather than a list of specific knowledge-based standards that serve to maintain Freire's "banking" concept of learning. It also requires that districts and schools assess results with more than standardized tests—that credence be given to student presentations, performances, and demonstrations as important indicators of achievement.

Portfolios can be helpful in documenting these products, and a representative sampling of them can be compared from year to year. Urban students must be freed from curriculum models that perpetuate their disenfranchisement. National and state standards fail to serve this goal if they focus on a positivist concept of learning that assumes students need "filling up" with

---

[3]In Lee (1999) I present what is primarily a liberal argument for standards that support democratic excellence and outline guidelines for developing such programs. However, these guidelines also support the need to address the critical theorist's concern for broadening the knowledge codes addressed by standards if democratic goals are to be realized.

mainstream knowledge to eliminate their learning deficits. The project-based, inclusionary model recommended here begins with the assumption that all students are intelligent and will become more so when they are engaged in sustained intellectual exploration. Such a curriculum serves the ideals of a democratic society by capitalizing on the richness of ethnic, social, and cultural differences in classrooms that promote a culture of quality.

REFERENCES

Alton-Lee, A., Nuthall, G., & Patrick, J. (1993). Reframing classroom research: A lesson from the private world of children. In E. Mintz & J. Yun (Eds.), *The complex world of teaching: Perspectives from theory and practice* (pp. 43–75). Cambridge, MA: Harvard Educational Review.

Aronoff, M. (1999, November 28). Words and rules. *New York Times Book Review*, p. 26.

Berger, R. (1996). *A culture of quality* (Occasional Paper Series, No. 1). Providence, RI: Annenberg Institute of School Reform, Brown University.

Chilcoat, G., & Ligon, J. (1999). "Helping to make democracy a living reality": The curriculum conference of the Mississippi Freedom Schools. *Journal of Curriculum and Supervision, 15*(1), 43–68.

Darling-Hammond, L. (1997). *The right to learn.* San Francisco: Jossey-Bass.

Freire, P. (1970). *Pedagogy of the oppressed.* New York: Herder & Herder.

Giroux, H.A. (1998). *Schooling and the struggle for public life: Critical pedagogy in the modern age.* Minneapolis: University of Minnesota Press.

Haberman, M. (1991, December). The pedagogy of poverty vs. good teaching, *Phi Delta Kappan*, pp. 290–294.

Hirsch, E.D. (1997). *Course knowledge sequence: Content guidelines for grades K-8.* Charlottesville: Core Knowledge Foundation.

Jorgensen, C. (1994/1995). Essential questions—inclusive answers. *Educational Leadership, 52*(4), 52–55.

Kanpol, B. (1995). Outcome-based education and democratic commitment: Hopes and possibilities. *Educational Policy, 9*(4), 359–374.

Kozol, J. (1991). *Savage inequalities.* New York: HarperCollins.

Lee, J. (1999). "Standards of excellence" in democratic classrooms: A description and critique of three philosophical approaches with a model for linking theory to practice. *The Journal of Critical Pedagogy, 3*(1). http://www.lib.wmc.edu/pub/jcp/issueIII1/contents.html.

McDonald, J., Rogers, B., & Sizer, T. (1993). *Standards and school reform: Asking the essential questions* (Studies on Exhibitions, No. 8). Providence: RI: Annenberg Institute for School Reform, Brown University.

Nieto, S. (1995). *Affirming diversity: The sociopolitical context of multicultural education* (2nd ed.). New York: Longman.

Ohanian, S. (1999). *One size fits few: The folly of educational standards.* Portsmouth, NH: Heinemann.

Resnick, L., & Hall, M. (1998). Learning organizations for sustainable education reform. *Daedalus*, 89-118.

School District of Philadelphia. (1998). *Curriculum frameworks*. Philadelphia, PA: Author.

Thompson, S. (1999, October 6). Confessions of a "standardisto." *Education Week*, p. 46.

Wiggins, G., & McTighe, J. (1998). *Understanding by design*. Alexandria, VA: Association for Supervision and Curriculum Development.

Yeo, F. (1997). *Inner-city schools, multiculturalism, and teacher education: A professional journey*. New York: Garland.

Zemelman, S., Daniels, H., & Hyde, A. (1998). *Best practice: New standards for teaching and learning in America's schools* (2nd ed.). Portsmouth, NH: Heinemann.

3

The Impact of Voice on the Politics of Inclusion in the Literacy Classroom

Mary DeKonty Applegate

Saint Joseph's University

Writing a chapter that focuses on the impact of the politics of inclusion on literacy has been a true catalyst for me. I began my undergraduate studies in the late 1950s when many educators cautioned against mixing politics and education. Many years later, I still find myself wishing that it were possible to keep educational issues separate from politics. This ideal exists despite the fact that I have seen political considerations consistently impact on the core of literacy pedagogy with positive as well as negative results. These political considerations, it seems, are always theoretically derived.

The history of literacy has been characterized by extreme swings from behavioral models to cognitive-sociological models. Pearson and Stevens (1996) presented an intellectual history of literacy instruction that reflects the impact of political factors on pedagogical and theoretical positions. For years, behaviorist models of literacy assumed the power position and controlled daily teaching practices. Several voices questioned a view of learning that placed learners in such a passive role. These voices had little influence for years. As greater and greater evidence mounted that questioned the passive role of the learner, cognitive and sociological models of literacy that emphasized human freedom and choice moved into a powerful political position. Many educators, wanting to identify with these newly perceived authorities, added their voices in support of these cognitive models. The idealist in me wanted to forget that politics was at work here.

Because of the political impact on literacy theory, however, over the years a wide range of literacy models, behavioral, cognitive, and critical, has been proposed. Despite the great variation that exists in the specifics of these models, most recognize three "players" in the process: the reader (or learner), the context, and the author. A second common thread among more recent literacy models is the realization that learners are active participants in the creation of their own understandings.

A parallel political/educational issue is that of inclusion. Inclusion for many people refers to the makeup of today's classrooms, in which children who were previously housed in special settings are now part of the regular classroom. This chapter does not focus on that generic aspect of inclusion; however, I do focus more on the issues of inclusion inherent in the urban classroom often composed of large numbers of minority students. I attempt to investigate the nature of the active learner and the way in which the voice of the learner can contribute to the dialogue that occurs among the reader, the context, and the author in the politics of inclusion.

Before I continue, I briefly summarize the concept of voice that I will use in this paper (Applegate & Goodman, 2002). Giroux (1988a), from a critical perspective, suggested that a student's voice is created through personal history, specifically those distinguishing experiences with the significant characters in her life who are also central to the individual's culture. He concluded that "voice, then, refers to the means at our disposal—the discourses available to use—to make ourselves understood and listened to, and to define ourselves as active participants in the world" (p. 199).

This concept of voice in literacy, therefore, is based on the assumption that effective readers can and indeed must play active roles in the construction of meaning in literacy; therefore, I need to consider the importance of the types of classroom that contribute to the creation of active learners. Consequently, I begin by examining the role of readers as active participants in the learning process. From there, I move to the classroom as the context of literacy; in doing so, I need to address the teacher's role in the dynamics of literacy learning. Furthermore, because I am using literacy as the vehicle for learning, I will need to give thoughtful consideration of the role of the third player, the author and/or the text, and the role of the text in fostering the interaction among all three players. I then explore the ways in which political insights can make positive inroads in the creation of included urban classrooms. Finally, after considering all players, I raise some possible ways in which an understanding of voice can positively impact on the politics of inclusion.

FIRST PLAYER: READERS

It is important that I begin by sharing the image that I have of ideal active, engaged readers. These readers are those who, with their peers, respond to text and, in the spirit of give and take, report how they used their experiences and ideas to create this response. They encourage others to do the same and to concur with or challenge their views. What is it that enables these readers to first create a mental picture of the text, to share that meaning-making process, and to willingly listen to confirmations or rejections of the images that they have created? I focus on the role of voice in that process. Giroux (1988a) suggested that readers' voices or identities serve as the vehicles that they have at their disposal to generate their understandings and to make themselves understood and listened to. They use these identities, or voices, to define themselves as active participants in the world. They then use their voices to accept or reject ideas based on the degree to which these ideas fit or contradict those they have developed with the significant community in their lives.

How are learners' voices created? McLaren (1997) suggested that the development of voice comes from a three-dimensional perspective: the functional, the cultural, and the critical. Although these can be discussed separately, they really cannot be disconnected. The functional voice is created through students' experiences, or histories, and determines the ways in which they use their voice to function (effectively or ineffectively) in their world. The second dimension of voice is created as learners use their cultural perspectives to mediate their historical or lived experiences. The critical voice refers to the unconscious will or force used by learners to mesh the historical and cultural voices while creating their own identities. Learners will use voice to critique ideas expressed in classrooms and to determine whether the assumptions underlying the ideas match with those they have created.

What is of particular importance here is that the idealized classroom experiences just described can now become part of the students' personal histories. Specifically, the discussions in which they are involved can enable the learners to connect their experiences with those of others, to compare and contrast these experiences, and to give credibility to the experiences of all. This type of literacy involvement becomes one of the many experiences used to create their identities. We can conclude that students' voices enabled their learning experiences and that their learning experiences now become part of the creation of voice. This suggests that as students participate in active learning experiences, their voices, or identities become stronger in the ability to positively impact on the learning experience of others.

In the less than ideal classroom, however, it is quite possible to meet students whose voices are not actively contributing to this cyclical learning process. Many urban youth bring voices to classrooms and do not find an environment that fosters their desires to respond to text. They do not perceive a spirit of give-and-take within the classroom that encourages them to use their experiences and ideas to respond to the ideas of others often they are simply presented with the ideas of others with little or no opportunity to question or bring into play their own experiences. Therefore, there is no encouragement of others to contribute to a give-and-take or to concur with or challenge their views. Thus, to Giroux and other critical theorists, the existence of democratic classrooms is crucial to the development of student voice and is contingent on teachers becoming more and more aware of the central role of students' voice in the development of literacy.

SECOND PLAYER: THE CONTEXT IN THE CLASSROOM

What type of a classroom allows students to use their own voices in learning? The answer to this question must address two separate issues: the classroom environment created by the teacher and the view of reading being embodied in the classroom. In addressing the classroom environment, Freire (1978/1982) suggested that four elements are essential for classrooms that value student voice:

> Organize classroom relationships so that students can draw on and confirm those dimensions of their own histories and experiences that are deeply rooted in the surrounding community, . . . assume pedagogical responsibility for attempting to understand the relationships and forces that influence students outside the immediate context of the classroom, . . . develop curricula and pedagogical practices around those community traditions, histories, and forms of knowledge that are often ignored within the dominant school culture, . . create the conditions where students come together to speak, to engage in dialogue, to share their stories, and to struggle together within social relations that strengthen rather than weaken possibilities for active citizenship. (pp. 199-201)

Although Freire (1978/1982) viewed the classroom as the structure for providing learners with an apprenticeship in democracy, he wanted teachers to understand that learners from subordinate cultures often submit to the ideas and realities endorsed by those representing the majority views. Later, Freire (1978/1982) provided insights that are more specific to the educational and political discrepancy between majority middle-class children and students belonging to various subordinate cultures. He suggested that teachers need to help students from subordinate cultures understand the sociopolitical functions of literacy that will determine the degree of participation that individual members can have in society. Dagostino and

Carifio (1994), in keeping with Freire, suggested that literature can become a vehicle to enable individuals to become valuable contributors who do not depend on society for their way of life. Willinsky (1990) emphasized the need for teachers to become engaged meaning-makers who are willing to take the political plunge needed to impact education's responsibility to a democratic society.

However, the prevalence of such critical reflection cannot be limited to the teachers' impact on schools and society. Unless it extends to the children whom we teach, we cannot hope to effect broad and permanent change. That is, unless children's learning occurs within classrooms that provide them with opportunities to reflect on their own meaning-making, the contributions of their experiences, and the validation of textual interpretation that comes about with the combining of text and experience, they cannot possibly value and reflect on the interpretation and experiences of others. This ability to reflect, learn, respect, and change is the core of the process of classroom democratization that promises to transform education in our society.

We have already noted that Freire (1978/1982) wanted teachers to understand that learners from subordinate cultures often submit to the ideas and realities of the main culture. We also noted his suggestion that teachers help students from subordinate cultures understand the sociopolitical functions of literacy. However, we need to take into account insights presented by Kanpol and Brady (1998) that refocus our attention to individual identities. Kanpol and Brady pointed out the fallacy of the assumption that there is a certain oneness of culture and experience that various subgroups draw on as they go about the process of meaning-making. In taking issue with the diversity label, they suggested that teachers consider the multifarious differences that individuals with various cultures bring to the classroom. These differences must be recognized and valued if classrooms are to be effective apprenticeships for democracy.

Dewey (1916/1944) long ago set the stage for connecting voice to classrooms by emphasizing the need for education to provide for all children, regardless of color, class, and gender, the opportunity for equity in our educational structures. In his earlier work, Dewey (1916/1944) was concerned about creating classrooms that afforded all members an equitable opportunity for participation. He proposed that

> all members of the group must have an equitable opportunity to receive and to take from others. There must be a large variety of shared undertakings and experiences. Otherwise, the influences which educate some into masters educate others into slaves. And the experience of each party loses in meaning when the free interchange of varying modes of life experiences is arrested. . . . (This) lack of free equitable intercourse which springs from a variety of shared interests make intellectual stimulation unbalanced. (pp. 84-85)

Willinsky (1990) suggested that equity in educational structures requires literacy advocates to raise society's awareness of the need for elevated levels of "literate participation and enfranchisement" (p. 20). Willinsky's challenge is that educators become willing to connect the personal and the political and to deal with the politics and power in literacy. Giroux (1988a) demonstrated his willingness to address this issue. To him, being literate is "not to be free, it is to be present and active in the struggle for reclaiming one's voice, history, and future" (p. 65). McLaren (1997) suggested that teachers use pedagogy that is situated in the intersection of language, culture, and history. All students need to be free to use their history, their language, and their culture. If not, students from subordinate cultures will be "denied a voice with which to be present in the world; they are made invisible to history and rendered powerless to shape it" (p. 223).

Giroux, McLaren, and Freire all emphasized the importance of creating a literacy classroom with a playing field that is equal for all participants, one that enables them to experience apprenticeship in a democratic structure. This will require that teachers recognize that individuals within each subgroup have unique experiences and assumptions about the world and that they will and should use these when interpreting the nature and actions of characters they meet in literature. All students need to be free to discuss their insights related to conflicts between and among characters; they need to know that their interpretations of conflicts that impact on characters resulting from societal pressures can be expressed and recognized as valid. They need to know that their interpretations will be treated with the same respect as those of the majority group. As students from subordinate cultures begin to experience a sense of respect from teachers and peers, they can begin the process of creating self-esteem within an environment in which they have traditionally experienced rejection. They can begin to use these experiences with literature to become part of their identities. They will experience the excitement of classrooms structured as workshops to further their intentions and meanings with their past, current, and future worlds beyond that depicted in the literature texts (Willinsky, 1990). They can, as suggested by Willinsky, understand literacy as the working of language in its written form. He proposed that the nature of the experience of literacy in the classroom is what constitutes an education. As Dewey (1988) suggested, "education which does not occur through forms of life, forms that are worth living for their own sake, is always a poor substitute for the genuine reality, and tends to cramp and deaden" (p. 169). In this way, literacy becomes the way to create a path between home and school, enabling all students to incorporate these classroom experiences into their personal identities.

CONTEXT—PART II: VIEW OF LITERACY

I believe that it is impossible to leave our discussion of the role of the classroom without addressing the view of literacy that is developed. Freire
(1978/1982) depicted a classroom in which literacy is presented from a skills
perspective when he coined the phrase *banking education*. Using this view
of reading, teachers "deposit" knowledge about words, sentences, and genre
into the empty accounts of students. The emphasis is on teachers making
deposits without finding whether the students can balance the checkbook or
ever use any of their factual capital to analyze or solve problems of importance to them. Freire's (1991) own account of teaching literacy best reflects
his position:

> I always saw teaching adults to read and write as a political act, an act of
> knowledge, and therefore a creative act. I would find it impossible to be
> engaged in a work of mechanically memorizing vowel sounds, as in the
> exercise "ba-be-bi-bo-bu, la-le-li-lo-lu." Nor could I reduce learning to
> read and write merely to learning words, syllables, or letters, a process
> of teaching in which the teacher *fills* the supposedly empty heads of
> learners with his or her words. On the contrary, the student is the sub-
> ject of the process of learning to read and write as an act of knowing and
> of creative. . . . Reading the world always precedes reading the word,
> and reading the word implies continually reading the world. . . . For this
> reason I have always insisted that words used in organizing a literacy
> program come from what I call the "word universe" of people who are
> learning, expressing their actual language, their anxieties, fears,
> demands, and dreams. Words should be laden with the meaning of the
> people's existential experience, and not of the teacher's experience.
> Surveying the word universe thus gives us the people's words, pregnant
> with the world, words from the people's reading of the world . . . all this
> was proposed to the students' curiosity in a dynamic and living way, as
> objects to be discovered within the body of texts, whether the student's
> own or those of established writers, and not as something stagnant
> whose outline I described. The students did not have to memorize the
> description mechanically, but rather learn its underlying significance.
> Only by learning the significance could they know how to memorize it,
> to fix it. (pp. 24-26)

It is clear that in order to foster active learning, students must be presented with a view of reading and writing that focuses on the importance of
connecting literacy to real life. To do so would require greater emphasis on
literacy as a social process. This would mean that classrooms need to become
workshops that furthers students' intentions and meanings with a world that
extends beyond textbooks and that enables learners to make something of
that world (Willinsky, 1990).

This suggests that the quality of discussion within the classroom is connected to the participants' understanding of literacy itself. Only when transacting with texts has a meaningful personal purpose will students become engaged in such a way that these classroom experiences now become part of the students' personal history. Specifically, the discussion must enable students to connect their experiences with those of others, to compare and contrast these experiences, and to give credibility to all experiences. In that way, learners can consider the classroom as one of many experiences used to create their identities. If not, the classroom will be viewed as something that is peripheral to their real lives.

THIRD PLAYER: WRITERS OR TEXTS

The third and final player in this discussion of voice and literacy is that of literacy itself: the writers or the storytellers and the text they create for the reader or listener to use to evoke meaning. Therefore, the discussion here is two-dimensional; I begin with an emphasis on literature as a concept and then move to the author's role in the creation of the text. Langer (1995) described several vignettes of students responding to literature. Again, in a spirit of give and take, they reported how they used their experiences and ideas to create their responses. They encouraged others to do the same and to concur with or challenge their views.

> They interiorize their various readings in a quest for personal meaning, examine the text and life to varying degrees from a critical perspective, and treat others' comments as having the potential to enrich (as well as challenge) their own understandings. They also know that they have the right to disagree and that they are likely to modify if not change their ideas with time. And so it is with literature. Solitary thought continues, and more public discussion is always possible. In a literary experience there are no ends, only pauses—and future possibilities. (p. 4)

It is very easy to understand why Langer suggested that literature is personal, social, and intellectual. To her, we use literature

> to explore both ourselves and others, to define and redefine who we are, who we might become, and how the world might be.... As we read and tell stories through the eyes of our imagined selves, our old selves gradually disappear from our recollections, our remembrances of yesterday become firmly rewritten, and our new selves take on a strength and permanence that we believe was and is who we are. All literature—the stories we read as well as those we tell—provides us with a way to imagine

human potential. In its best sense, literature is intellectually provocative as well as humanizing, allowing us to use various angles of vision to examine thoughts, beliefs, and actions. (p. 5)

What I find thrilling is that once again, as we focus our attention on one player, the text, we see that it is impossible to separate either the reader or the context from this exciting process. Literature as the opportunity for exploring ourselves and others cannot happen in classrooms where students are passively dissecting parts of text focusing on ideas proposed by others with no connection to their lives or needs.

Rosenblatt (1938/1968) believed that the literary experience is dependent on both head and heart and that this experience parallels life. The experience of literature relates to the needs of individuals who experience the conflicts and stresses of life; to Rosenblatt, literary experiences could serve as the core of the type of educational experiences needed for a democracy.

If we only do justice to the potentialities inherent in literature itself, we can make a vital social contribution. As the student vicariously shares through literature the emotions and aspirations of other human beings, he can gain heightened sensitivity to the needs and problems of others remote from him in temperament, in space, or in social environment; he can develop a greater imaginative capacity to grasp the meaning of abstract laws or political and social theories for actual human lives. Such sensitivity and imagination are part of the indispensable equipment of the citizen of a democracy. (p. 274)

Goodman (1985) noted the political role of the text; written language was created because a community recognized its interdependence in trade and political structures with other communities. He also noted the role of text in preserving a culture when oral traditions could no longer preserve a culture by passing it on to upcoming generations. He emphasized the connection between written language and personal and social developments. Goodman also pointed out that texts are shaped by both the writer's view of the readers as writer's own characteristics. He pointed out the following:

in every act of writing, writers are constrained by their own values, their concepts, the experiences they have had and the schemata they have built of them. The purpose of the particular text being created will always be influenced by these personal characteristics of the writer, so that the text will reflect when the writer is as well as what the writer is trying to communicate. (p. 816)

Probably one of the most essential aspects to include in responding to literature, is that of helping students recognize the assumptions that the writers of text have about the characters, their actions, and conflicts and their ways to resolve conflicts. As students learn that responding to literature includes a critique of these assumptions, they can begin to experience some control over their own learning. This can have a significant impact on their willingness to begin to identify with the class, with the discussion and possibly with the characters. In short, they can become an integral part of the democratic structure that can exist in the classroom. Rosenblatt (1938/1968) demonstrated a deep commitment to the view that through literature, students could become better able to explore human relations and that this exploration could enable them to promote the democratic ideals so crucial to Dewey.

USING VOICE TO SYNTHESIZE THE THREE PLAYERS

Giroux (1988a) suggested that the readers' voices are their identities, which they use to generate their understandings and to make themselves understood and listened to. They, as readers, use these identities to define themselves as active participants in the world. They also use their voices to accept or reject ideas based on the degree to which these fit or contradict those they have developed with the significant community in their lives. Hynds (1990) pointed out the significance of context in the creation of voice:

> Readers operate within a context of social perspective, including their conceptions of teachers' expectations, the value placed on reading by peers and significant adults, and their own notions of themselves as readers. (p. 250)

In the classroom context, students use their voices to respond to authors and the texts they create. Hynds pointed out that readers use their social perspectives in the classroom and in their world, using these notions as the basis for learning to "construe the underlying motivations and thoughts of characters in the text world" (p. 250). Voice then, becomes the magnet that pulls together the reader, the context in which reading occurs, and the writer, or text used during reading. Hopefully, the instructional context of reading, a classroom that is structured to enhance the learners' potential to make a positive contribution to our democratic process, fosters the creation of change within all three players, the readers, the texts and the context. Because of this change, readers learn to develop voices that will enable them to use the power of language and the knowledge they possess to change and improve the quality of their lives (Freire, 1978/1982).

Rosenblatt (1938/1968) believed that a liberal education would provide potential literature teachers with the tools and the knowledge they would

need to help students objectively critique those ideas and opinions generally accepted by the society. To her, literature could provide the underpinning
of a liberal education, and could therefore foster the type of critical thinking
needed to fulfill that constitutional dream of a government that was by, of
and for its people. It is important that we take a deeper look into how
Rosenblatt believed this could happen.

Pradl (1991) noted that during Rosenblatt's term as editor-in-chief of
the *Bernard Bulletin* from April 1923 to April 1924, she participated in the
debate related to students' responsibility for taking an active role in their
own education. She was strongly influenced by Dewey's concern about the
way in which a laissez-faire structure could hinder students' development of
self-expression. Pradl suggested that it was that fear that sparked
Rosenblatt's editorial of March 28, 1924:

> The student cannot spend sixteen or eighteen years in . . . habit forma-
> tion and then expect habits of intellectual freedom to suddenly appear.
> If intellectual curiosity and freedom are to be the dominating principles
> of higher education they must be equally prevalent in the lower schools.
> (p. 25)

Rosenblatt was clearly influenced by Dewey's view that children's intellectual curiosity is to be encouraged throughout their entire school life, but
Rosenblatt applied this notion specifically to the teaching of literature. The
result is reflected in her view that intellectual exploration of literature must
include a two-dimensional voice development: the private reader and the
public participant in dialogue (1938/1968). The private reader lives through
and reflects on the "lives" of characters and "vicariously shares their struggles and perplexities and achievements. He becomes a part of strange environments, or he sees with new emotions the conditions and the lives about
him" (p. 174). This private process is the result of a transaction between the
private *self* of the individual's mind and the literary work that the reader uses
to elicit "a vivid personal response" (p. 175). This is a private process of imagining the human implications of any situation. Rosenblatt noted that if "our
imaginations functioned actively, nowhere in the world would there be children who were starving. Our vicarious suffering would force us to do something to alleviate their plight" (p. 176). To Rosenblatt, this private response
resulted as the individual used literature as a means of exploring and celebrat-
ing human experience. The reader's interpretation was based on the total self
and funneled through words that represent their own "sensuous, emotion,
and intellectual perceptions" (p. 49). This is clearly a very private experience.

However, the power of Rosenblatt's insights is reflected in the balance
she described between the private self with the public response. This public
participation or self-expression involved a classroom filled with private

selves who needed to hear different reactions and experiences seen through another's vision. This public dialogue enables readers to hear how others used their understanding of the human condition to evoke their interpretations. Rosenblatt wanted this public dialogue to consider the "basic human traits that persist despite social and cultural changes. To what extent are the resemblances of one age to another, as well as the differences, due to environmental influences? Indeed, this question of persisting or 'universal' human traits is one that arises constantly in discussions of literature" (p. 12). She observed that learners often unquestioning adopt society's view of human nature and conduct. Consequently, the public dialogue provides the opportunity to question this "voluntaristic" view of human motivation by replacing it with a "keener sense of the complexities in the many environmental, physiological, and involuntary psychological factors that influence behavior (p. 15). Hopefully, the public dialogue will negate any conclusions the private self created based solely on her or his "own meager experience and casually acquired assumptions" (p. 15).

We can see in Rosenblatt a balance between the personal and the political; to her, reading literature was "an individual and unique occurrence" that happened as the reader was engaged in a private and aesthetic experience with the text. However, this individually fulfilling response to literature was also linked with a social dimension that enables the reader to work out "a basis for a more fruitful living" (p. 212). As readers used books to leave their "particular limited cultural group" (p. 228), they would become aware of the social and psychological needs of the citizens in this democratic society. Here we see Rosenblatt's interest in literature's role in fostering a balance between education and social and political awareness.

Thus, there appears to be a balance between the private process of reading and the changes that can occur in one's private self as a result of public dialogue; thus, we can see the public consequence of reading. We can picture readers then as having private selves and public selves. The private self involves the ability to use their voices to act on text to create their personal picture of text; they then need to reflect on their own meaning-making and the contributions of their experiences and they contrast their own with those reported by others. The classroom provides the opportunity for students to share these ideas with others; this reflects the public self. The public selves of readers must experience a contextual validation of their textual interpretations that come about with the combining of text and experience; they cannot possibly value and reflect on the interpretation and experiences of others. Thus, the balancing of the private and public selves fosters the ability to reflect, learn, respect, and change and is the core of the process of classroom democratization that promises to transform education in our society.

We can turn to Rosenblatt to gain insights into the way in which literature and the classroom play a role in the creation of private and public selves.

She continually presents the literary experience as part of the literature class-room that furthers "the assimilation of habits of thought conducive to social understanding" (p. 22). Furthermore, she connects the commitment to one's public self a central part of our democratic structure; to her, our democratic structure is a function of the quality of life and the relationships earned among its members and not dispensed dogmatically from above. The private self, or the critical thinker, requires that learners be sensitive to the "insecurity, this craving for some easy, reassuring formula," that can result in blind following. The private self must develop one's faith in one's own judgments while continuing to hold these judgments open to question. The critical thinking associated with one's private self resists treating belief as dogma to be imposed on others. Clearly, Rosenblatt's treatment of linking literature with the classroom, with viewing literature as a work of art, and with recog-nizing that through literature students will learn to reach outward to the social context of other readers reflect the way in which learners develop the type of private and public selves needed for effective participation in a democracy.

Langer (1995) provided additional insights into the ways in which liter-ature enhances the development of private and public selves. She emphasized literature as a medium for (a) learning from and communicating with our-selves and others and (b) reflecting on our lives, our choices, and the human condition. Literature helps build on home discourse and can contribute toward helping learners develop meaning, self-esteem, and experiences with thoughtfulness. The public selves can be enhanced through small group dis-cussions where students take ownership for their interpretations and reac-tions during the discussion and where teachers provide support for their developing insights, to explore horizons of possibilities and to use the social-interactive context as well as the text to explore ideas. Teachers need to help students see themselves as adept language and literacy learners who are reflecting a school learning that follows closely and builds on the literacy learning they acquired outside of school. Teachers' responsibility is to iden-tify the ways in which they are learning the literate thinking strategies most often associated with academic success. Teachers must also ensure that they are asking probing questions that are promoting high-level thinking that requires an integration of students' experiences and text.

If Rosenblatt's concept of the study of literature via public classroom dialogue were regularly implemented, then the classroom would have the potential to become another of Giroux's significant communities in the lives of students. Under such circumstances, children would no longer have to accept or reject ideas based on how well they fit with their existing notions. Instead, voice would grow through an ultimately dynamic exchange of ideas within Hynds' (1990) broader context, a community of learners in the lan-guage arts classroom.

VOICE IN THE URBAN CLASSROOM

"Many urban children come to school hungry, abused, and/or poorly clothed. They come to school from communities distinguished by empty buildings, boarded-up shops, proliferating liquor stores, random violence, pent-up anger and dehumanizing marginalization, poverty, and self-inflicted crime" (Yeo, 1997, p. 202). These are the experiences that they use to create their functional, cultural, and critical voices.

The significance of the connections between politics and literacy impacts most strongly on urban youth. If literacy is the vehicle through which learners learn who they are, then meaning-making for learners from the various subordinate cultures will be significantly different from that of learners from the majority. Learners who do not see themselves in the texts they read soon get the message that some things are for others but not for them. They look around and see the significant others in their world unemployed or with low-entry jobs and that reinforces the message as to who they are. They hear about the national tests that people use to make judgments about their academic worth and add that to their view of themselves. This low self-esteem impacts on the expectations they have for themselves and their peers. This rather bleak picture becomes the meaning-making vessel they bring to the classrooms. The ideas they have about themselves will become the mental building blocks they use for meaning making in the classroom, even if they are fortunate enough to participate in a classroom where meaning making is valued. Without a teacher who is sensitive to the need to alter that message, to use texts with characters with whom these children can identify, and to use literacy in authentic ways, these learners may never reach their meaning-making potential. Instead, many will soon experience this self-fulfilling prophecy and become another statistic to support the conclusion that they along with others in their community represent a deficit in learning and growth. But rather than allow ourselves to be overwhelmed by pessimism, we must recognize that urban classrooms represent enormous opportunities to impact positively on the lives of children.

Hopefully, these same classrooms will foster opportunities for children to use insights gained through private and public transactions with meaningful literature to identify with characters who overcome life's obstacles and become empowered to impact their own futures. These students need literature teachers who appreciate public dialogues that allow for differences in interpretations of the actions of characters that occur in a spirit of social cooperation and community life. The public dialogue in these classrooms will enable readers to make changes in their private awareness of literature and the learning it provides about opportunities within society.

The urban community provides the setting that the students, as characters, use as they create the stories in their lives. Literature enables them to experience the lives of people in different settings and to apply the learning experiences of the characters to their private selves. This setting sets the scene for urban youth to explore themselves and others, to define and redefine who they are, who they might become, and how their world might be. Thomas and Flint (1987) investigated the options available to urban students and concluded that students' perceptions of what is available to them will determine their definitions of reality. These definitions will in turn serve as the basis for meaning-making in the literature classroom. Thomas and Flint challenged urban educators to provide cognitive and interpersonal experiences within the classroom that will improve urban youths' definition of reality regarding their future lives. We can take significant steps toward meeting this challenge if we structure the classroom and teacher expectations in the following ways.

Maximizing Opportunities Presented in the Urban Classroom

Help Learners Develop Literacy Skills. Learners need to be exposed to literature selections that will enable them to recognize the possibilities of using their own literacy as the means to transport themselves and others in their subculture into the mainstream. In order for them to achieve that goal, learners must be willing to and teachers must expect them to expend the energy they need to develop their literacy skills beyond their current level.

Learners Must Take Risks. Learners will have to discover the need to take risks, to view the world as one that is possible to change, and to recognize the possibilities they have for creating choices instead of completely accepting the status quo. It is important to recognize, as Dagostino and Carifio (1994) point out, for some the risk might be too great and the struggle too difficult; for them, literacy presented a responsibility that they did not anticipate and therefore, the literacy they acquired will not result in a liberating power.

Public Dialogue. Often, students from various subordinate cultures are in classrooms taught by teachers from the main culture. These teachers must recognize the value of public dialogue. They must take to heart the insights of Dewey (1916/1944) that schools are the primary vehicles for creating learners' insights regarding democracy. They must understand that democracy requires its members to feel a moral obligation to establish a sense of community and struggle that ensures freedom and liberty for all its members. Freire (1978/1982), in arguing for an educational climate that fostered open dialogue, suggested that through class participation students become engaged with their world and develop a genuine sense of community. As mentioned earlier, Giroux (1988a) proposed that it is the students' voice, their personal and cultural identities that provides the basis for constructing and demonstrating the essence of a democratic society. Again, we are reminded of Rosenblatt's (1938/1968) account of the responsibility of the teacher to help readers become aware of the potential literacy brings in exploring the human condition, the outer world, and other ways of life. Readers need to know that through literacy we can gain human insight and initiate fulfilling explorations into the problems of life and the process of creating and implementing solutions.

Let Students Know You Care. Teachers need to let students know that they care about them as people and about their future. They need to use the fullness of the human experience to stretch the public dialogue beyond the students' present perceptions. For example, when a literary experience generates discussion about a character's poor decision making, a teacher can connect that to ways in which people in today's society use credit cards that result in exorbitant interest rates added to the cost of items. Discussion can also be connected to gullible individuals who accept misleading statements about candidates in elections. In this way, the teacher is using literature to help students develop as participants in a world in flux where dialogue is inevitable and where questions about decision making are crucial. They are being prepared to deal in a world where choices and healthy struggles are available for all those who have paid the price to participate (Dagostino & Carifio, 1994).

Assess the Issues of Power and Control. Darder (1991) cautioned teachers to be in tune to the possibilities that students from underrepresented communities become oppositional in their resistance to the dominant message of knowledge that they consider to be in conflict with their cultural voice. This can happen even in classrooms where teachers are attempting to create conditions for cultural democracy. Because of this, it is extremely important that teachers assess the issues of power and control constructs that may have unconsciously incorporated into their private self as reader and participant in public dialogue. This can easily apply to a balance between required reading and choice reading. The teacher, as the representative of power, can exemplify that the voices of students, as subordinate groups, can be valued. In this way, students experience first hand the realization that as they participate in a community they can have a voice in the decisions of that community; thus they are learning the dynamics of political systems. This needs to be contrasted with failure to participate within a political system and therefore losing a voice. It is very easy to imagine how the judicious use of specific literature selections can reinforce this type of discussion.

LEARNING THE POLITICS OF INCLUSION
IN THE LITERATURE CLASSROOM

If we can achieve the goals just outlined, what is it that students can learn? If these classrooms provide students with the opportunity for the self-expression needed to discuss their interpretations and to question the inter-pretations of others, they begin to experience a sense of control in their own learning. This process, however, must be one in which a thorough under-standing of literature is being developed so that they are growing as learn-ers. It is worth revisiting Rosenblatt to review some of the implications that we can derive regarding the private self as a reader and the knowledge base used to create a response.

Pradl (1991) noted that Rosenblatt's inaugural editorial promised a pub-lication that would challenge students to become "more active, intelligence and constructive" (p. 26). What I focus attention on here is her belief in the pursuit of learning driven by a commitment to academic rigor that comes through in her editorial. She uses literature as the vehicle for this develop-ment and I suggest that part of the teacher's responsibility during the public dialogue that follows reading is to continually stretch students' knowledge base about literature itself. We need to create classrooms in which students thrill to an openness to new ideas because they realize that these new insights can be applied to their lives as well as to their next reading. They also recognize that their private interpretation will now be based on a wider knowledge base than the previous ones because of the new knowledge they have about literature and writers and the insights they acquired by listening to reactions and perceptions of their peers. What do urban youth need to bring to the literature experience so that it provides them with the opportu-nity to perceive themselves as being able to make a change in their lives and in their communities?

Dagostino and Carifio (1994) considered the answer as coming from both the community and its members. They proposed that the expectations and the goals of literacy education need to change as a society changes and makes new demands on its members. These members, in order to become participants in the society, are required to acquire multiple proficiencies.

> The ability to participate in local or national affairs or to move from one community to another requires a person to be literate enough not to be dependent on others for his or her way of life. Without sufficient liter-acy a person must trust that his or her quality of life will be guarded and promoted by others in the community. (p. 2)

To that end, they present literacy as consisting of five spheres. I briefly con-sider each sphere and the expectations that would be placed on urban youth based on each of these spheres.

The first sphere, or functional literacy, provides learners with "specific technical, almost mechanical skills reading, writing, and speaking" (p. 4). These are the skills that are usually assessed on standardized reading measures.

> The sphere of functional literacy is an environment where acceptable, minimal skills in reading and writing are at their most conceptually inane levels, perhaps almost devoid of intellectual and political content or cultural values. (p. 4)

Clearly this sphere is based on classrooms with teachers using the banking system referred to by Freire (1978/1982) in which students, as empty vessels need to be filled with facts and knowledge by teachers. This type of setting violates virtually every aspect of the classroom that we have established as our context. Based on the assumptions of active learning that we have proposed, we simply cannot ask children to suspend thinking and meaning-making until they have developed a set of skills. Fundamental reading skills must be viewed by students as tools that, when mastered, can help them create more complex meaning and develop both their private and public selves. Thus, the acquisition of functional knowledge is developed in a meaningful setting that enables students to see first hand the power that language has in the hands of the writer.

The second sphere, specialized literacy, enables learners to assimilate into a group that has common work and language; we often view this language as jargon! Examples of these specialized literacies are related to the worlds of computers, military, scientific, legal, and so on; nonetheless, students who will be successful with the demands of participation in the modern world will have sufficient literacy awareness so as to enable them to communicate within these groups.

> People who do not have a sense of this world and the language needed to function in it may be limited to their own environment which is most likely that of functional literacy. An unevenness of skills in different areas begins to emerge at this stage. As our society becomes more specialized, even extremely well-educated individuals will have a difficult time developing various specialized literacies as defined by this second sphere. (p. 5)

How can this specialized literacy be developed in our urban classroom?

I believe that this type of literacy is somewhat removed from the literature classroom but with one exception—that of the computer. Literature students need to be provided with word processors to be used as an integral part of their learning. As their insights are altered as a result of their participation in public dialogue, they can edit their responses used for group discussion and can experience first hand the speed at which the editing process can occur. But most importantly, as students express questions as to the intent or techniques of the writer, they can move to the internet for chat room dialogue with authors. What a thrilling experience this is! The understanding of terminology associated with the internet and with computers in general in included in the specialized literacy to which Dagostino and Carifio (1994) referred.

The third sphere, cultural and multicultural literacy, is often

> the sphere of the past, the comfortable, the sanctioned, the books remembered as a child, the lessons learned in youth by reactionary school reformers. Books for intellectual and social mobility are the fare. Cultural literacy is often the literacy of the academy. Multicultural literacy is a broader view of cultural literacy which enriches our lives and our relationships because it promotes the ideas and texts of minority groups. Minority groups share with the majority group the right to live beyond a survival level or within the confines of a caste system. (p. 6)

Clearly, Dagostino and Carifio (1994) presented a challenge to the teachers in our urban classrooms. Teachers need to balance the literature of the academy, often considered the classics of western civilization, with that from multiple cultures so that many cultures are recognized and function simultaneously. What is key here is that both types of literatures must be woven into one curriculum without creating the sense that one is superior to the others.

To Rosenblatt (1995), the human connection with other humans is central to the literacy experience.

> Although we may see some characters as outside ourselves . . . we are nevertheless able to enter into their behavior and their emotions. Thus it is that the youth may identify with the aged, one sex with the other, a reader of a particular limited social background with members of a different class or a different period. (p. 40)

This cannot happen in the creation of multicultural respect without a curriculum that balances the traditional cultural literacy with that of multicultural literature. The teacher in the urban classroom needs to be a central part of the public dialogue to ensure that learners do not internalize an expectation to merely accept the values, linguistic forms, and content of classic literature and reject the values, linguistic forms, and content of diverse literatures. Students need to see that literatures that reflect their identities are treated with equal respect and value.

The fourth sphere, critical literacy, has as its goal the potential to challenge individuals or groups to understand the complexities of participation in the mainstream.

> The sphere of critical literacy brings the potential for enlightenment and responsibility as well as for chaos and change. The goal is to educate students to participate in society as active, informed and critical citizens who can recognize oppressive and repressive forces in a society at large and who seek equity and democratic process in their lives . . . introduces students to various and perhaps opposing ideologies, social practices, and cultural forms . . . a world in flux, where dialogue is inevitable and questioning exchanges unavoidable . . . balanced around the tension of power struggles. . . . It is a world of choices and healthy struggle for many rather than judgment and oppression by a few. (p. 7)

What does this mean to the students in urban classroom? To me, this is a reflection of students' self-expression created by intellect and effort as evidenced during the public dialogue following reading. The classroom has become a microcosm of the larger society; students have participated in learning experiences in which their views have been valued. These students have been exposed to literature in which they could identify with the characters. They have interacted with characters from different cultures and different times and they have approved of or disagreed with the behaviors of these characters. They have noted similarities of the human condition and they have learned how characters who wanted a part of creating change went about making change. They now have to decide what they will do with that learning.

However, this critical perspective can not be achieved solely via teacher discourse; students have to discover the way in which characters choose or reject to work with those in power to make changes. Once again, they need to use the vehicle of literature to encourage them to make connections between their settings, conflicts, and solutions and those of the characters about whom they read. Hopefully, their literature world has demonstrated that those characters who were able to bring about change in their lives often learned how to effectively work with those in power who were capable of contributing to change. They come face to face with the possibility that a principle that they consciously developed may have to be altered into order to become an effective change agent for their lives and communities. They are learning the power of language as a political tool; they discover that some characters use this tool effectively and others never reach their potential because of an unwillingness to make the changes needed for its effective use.

The final sphere, the composite world, is one in which the mature reader is flexible, moving from the expectations of functional or specialized to cultural and critical literacy as is demanded by the situation.

The goal in a composite world is to produce a reader who is flexible and can function in any part of a composite world. The demands in a composite world are great. The reader is called on to be functionally literate, to comprehend specialized vocabulary, and to handle the demands of the cultural and multicultural sphere, and eventually that of critical literacy. . . . The composite sphere is a world of high intellectual or experiential demands as well as basic skills. The written word has the potential to be negotiable and questioned. (p. 8)

I believe that the urban classroom needs to be the students' composite sphere; students learn here to negotiate with those individuals who represent the voice of power. They need to be exposed to ways of reading and writing that enable them to experience the thrill of learning, to identify with or reject characters in stories, and to have their rationales valued. They need to be active participants who learn to negotiate a respect for differences in interpretations to stories.

If they have these experiences, they can use them to change their identifies from individuals who are helpless and disenfranchised to those who have possibilities for contributing to change. They will have learned that through negotiations and language they have effectively caused individuals who represent power to respect the position that they have presented. Because they have been included in the class dialogue, they understand the importance of expanding the range of those potentials, moving from the classroom to the school and from the school to the community. The range of possibilities continually widens as one understands how accepting the challenge of participation generates successful interactions and very positive experiences with inclusion.

CONCLUSION

Teachers who understand the power of students' voices in responding to literature can provide urban youth firsthand experiences with the excitement and responsibilities associated with inclusion in a community. This is especially significant to those students who feel disenfranchised from the main society. However, before they can see the possibility of changing their status within the main society, they need to experience the give and take of negotiating with those individuals who represent authority and consequently hold the power. In this classroom, they are provided with the opportunity to negotiate the curriculum, to select literature that reflects their personal needs and interests while accepting those selections that are assigned by the teacher. They become aware of the importance of balancing their private and the public conversations to expand the base of experiences they use in forming their identities. Through literature urban youth can go beyond their limited world and discover different worlds with different ways to solve problems. They need to experience the give and take that enables them to respect their insights, those of their peers, and the intellectual stretching brought about by probing questions from the teacher. Their voice needs to be valued before such use of self-expression can occur.

Thus, the voice that we use in the construction of meaning in response to text extends far beyond a mere literal recall of the details of a plot. And it is the recognized variations in the human experience that distinguishes us, challenges us, and, in the final analysis, forces us to grow. If the respect for these variations and the process through which we share them is nurtured in the urban classroom, it holds out unlimited promise for the growth and social contributions of its members. The challenge that faces urban students, teachers, and communities alike is to have faith in the human dimensions of mutual respect and growth as the key to fostering the principles of a democratic society.

But it would be unwise to consider voice as a static set of values or ideas related to one's social context. Reading must be viewed as a dynamic transaction that occurs between the author and reader, a transaction that can change both the reader and the reader's interpretation of the text. The literacy classroom holds out that same potential for its members. If teachers promote a mutual respect for the contributions of all members of the class, then the class itself could become another of Giroux's significant communities, those groups of people who help to form our ideas and values and through which we can see a clearer and better world.

REFERENCES

Applegate, M.D., & Goodman, M. (2002). Urban education: A critical theory of compassion and social justice. In B. Kanpol (Ed.), *Teacher education and urban education* (pp. 101-127). Cresskill, NJ: Hampton Press.

Dagostino, L., & Carifio, J. (1994). *Evaluative reading and literacy: A cognitive view.* Boston, MA: Allyn & Bacon.

Darder, A. (1991). *Culture and power in the classroom: A critical foundation for bicultural education.* Westport, CT: Bergin & Garvey.

Dewey, J. (1944). *Democracy and education.* New York: Macmillan. (Original work published 1916)

Dewey, J. (1988). My pedagogic creed. In S. Brown & M. Finn (Eds.), *Readings from progressive education: A movement and its professional journal* (Vol. 1, pp. 169-170). Lanham, MD: University Press of America. (Original work published 1897)

Freire, P. (1982). *Education for critical consciousness.* New York: Continuum. (Original work published 1978)

Freire, P. (1991). The importance of the act of reading. In B. Power & R. Hubbard (Eds.), *Literacy in process*. Portsmouth, NH: Heinemann.

Giroux, H. (1988a). *Teachers as intellectuals*. New York: Bergin & Garvey.

Goodman, K. (1985). Unity in reading. In H. Singer & R. Ruddell (Eds.), *Theoretical models and processes of reading* (3rd ed., pp. 813-840). Newark, DE: International Reading Association.

Hynds, S. (1990). Reading as a social event: Comprehension and response in the text, classroom, and world. In D. Bogdan & S. Shaw (Eds.), *Beyond communication: Reading comprehension and criticism* (pp. 237-256). Portsmouth, NH: Boynton/Cook.

Kanpol, B., & Brady, J. (1998). Teacher education and the multicultural dilemma: A "critical" thinking response. *Journal of Critical Pedagogy*.

Langer, J. (1995). *Envisioning literature: Literary understanding and literature instruction*. Teachers College, Columbia University.

McLaren, P. (1997). *Life in schools: An introduction to critical pedagogy in the foundations of education*. New York: Longman

Pradl, G. (1991). Reading literature in a democracy: The challenge of Louise Rosenblatt. In J. Clifford (Ed.), *The experience of reading: Louise Rosenblatt and reader-response theory* (pp. 21-26). Portsmouth, NH: Boynton/Cook.

Rosenblatt, L.M. (1995). *Literature as exploration*. New York: The Modern Language Association of America. (Original work published 1938 and 1968)

Thomas, J., & Flint, D. (1990). Black youth in urban schools: Attention, self concept and performance. *The State of Black Philadelphia, 9*, 37-48.

Willinsky, J. (1990). *The new literacy, redefining reading and writing in the schools*. New York: Routledge.

Yeo, F. (1997). *Urban education, multiculturalism and teacher education*. New York: Garland.

4

Multiculturalism
in Teacher Education

Philosophical Frameworks
and Teaching Models
for Transformative Learning

James O. Lee

Saint Joseph's University

Leaders in the field of multicultural education generally agree that little significant progress has been made in developing teaching practices and curriculum that meet the needs of inclusive classrooms that are culturally, racially, and socially diverse (Grant & Sleeter, 1994).

The research shows that most teachers display similar teaching practices that fail to address the diverse learning styles that exist in such classrooms (Cuban, 1984; Darder, 1991; Everhart, 1983; Goodlad, 1984; Grant & Sleeter, 1987; Kanpol & McLaren, 1995; Nieto, 1996; Sleeter, 1992; Yeo, 1997a). Issues of equity and excellence with respect to a diverse student population are assumed by many teachers to be non-issues, whether they teach in urban or suburban schools. In fact, in suburban schools in which the population in basically White and middle class, the need for multicultural education is often viewed as unnecessary. As one assistant superintendent in a rather well-off school district in Pennsylvania put it when asked about the usefulness of multicultural workshops for her staff, "We don't need any of that as we don't have too many minorities and most of our teaching staff is White." Ironically, this school district's vision statement embodied an inclusive philosophy, included teaching about and promoting diversity.

School districts such as this one, with little cultural and racial diversity within its student body and teaching staff, are usually ill equipped to achieve the goals of inclusive, multicultural education, even when well intentioned. Moreover, the assumption that multicultural education is only important if the school district's population is itself diverse represents a misunderstanding of the importance of providing all students, especially those who have been raised with strong Anglocentric cultural and social values, with the understandings and competencies necessary to contribute to achieving the goal of a democratic, multicultural society.

Within the multicultural literature, Banks (1944) defined the goal of multicultural education as that of helping students to "develop cross-cultural competency within the American national culture, with their own subculture and within and across different subsocieties and cultures" (p. 9). The development of such competency involves knowledge of cultural and racial differences and issues; the critical examination of one's own beliefs and values regarding culture, race, and social class; and an understanding of how knowledge, beliefs, and values determine one's behavior with respect to minority groups. In its more critical form, cross-cultural competency can promote the development of students who are social reformers, working for a more just and democratic society in which power and resources are more equitably distributed, much like Saltman argued for in chapter 2.

However, unless educators are themselves cross-culturally competent, students will not become so, at least not as the result of their schooling. A majority of teachers are White and middle class, monolingual, and bring little intercultural experience from their largely suburban and small-town backgrounds. Additionally, they often uncritically accept ability tracking, forms of traditional instruction that appeal to a narrow range of learning styles, and curricula whose content excludes minority groups. Many do not believe that minority students are capable of learning high-level concepts or achieving excellence, subscribing, instead, to a compensatory, skill-and-drill approach to learning. They often assume that decisions about what is important for students to know and how it can best be taught are culturally neutral issues and that there are generic principles of good teaching that apply regardless of cultural context. Typically, they do not examine the cultural content of their curriculum and pedagogy that may give preferential treatment to students whose cultural backgrounds are most like school norms. LaBelle's (1976) examples are helpful here:

> The way . . . in which the teacher responds to student behavior, the often control mechanisms, the topics and issues chosen for classroom study,

the schedule of activities in terms of the amount of subtle distinctions made between the sexes, the nature of the classroom time devoted to particular aspects of the school day, the spatial organization of the classroom, and the rewards and punishments meted out are . . . cultural loaded and . . . transmit messages [that] reinforce certain student behaviors and discourage others. (pp. 67-82)

Some will find this indictment of educators too harsh. They will point to programs already in the schools whose goal is multicultural education, even in suburban, middle class, largely Anglo schools. Nevertheless, as seen here many of these programs reflect a conservative or liberal approach to the topic that fails to promote inclusive education or teach students to be cross-culturally competent. They are "exposed" to cosmetic efforts that fail to address the culpability of the dominant culture in perpetuating inequity and do not provide students with the knowledge and skills necessary to work for a more just society.

Because schools are ill prepared to support Banks' (1994) goal of multicultural education and often lack the interest and commitment to change, the importance of teacher education at the preservice level becomes paramount. Teacher education programs in colleges and universities must make the commitment to encouraging the kind of transformative learning in preservice educators that eventually will result in powerful multicultural programs for students. Preservice teachers must learn, for example, how to use culturally sensitive strategies and content; to recognize the cultural underpinnings of their own logic and thought, as well as those of others; and to understand how cultural and linguistic differences may explain what in the past have been labeled as learning disabilities. Only in this way will they enter the profession able to provide equitable opportunities for academic success, personal development, and individual fulfillment for all students.

In too many cases, however, prospective teachers are still being prepared to teach in "idealized schools that serve white, monolingual, middle-class children from homes with two parents" (Ladson-Billings, 2000, pp. 86-87). King (1991) described many of these teachers as possessing a *dysconscious* racism, defining the term as "an uncritical habit of mind (including perceptions, attitudes, assumptions, and beliefs) that justifies inequity and exploitation by accepting the existing order of things as given" (p. 135). The literature is also clear that multicultural issues are rarely addressed in the supervision of preservice teachers (Zeichner & Hoeft, 1996). Recent studies of student teaching conclude that the role of supervisors is usually limited to the facilitation of the student teachers' assimilation into the school culture and traditional teaching practices. Supervisors are not viewed as responsible for helping student teachers question accepted practices and attitudes of the schools in which they teach (Britzman, 1991; Feiman-Nemser & Buchmann, 1985; Richardson-Koehler, 1988). Instead, instrumental issues of teaching technique and classroom management dominate the supervisory agenda without time devoted to examining the social and cultural values that often influence instructional decisions. Moreover, there is a lack of literature providing guidelines on how to raise the cultural consciousness of both student teachers and supervisors regarding inclusive instructional practice in multicultural classrooms (Apt-Perkins, Hauschildt, & Dale, 2000).

Of course, multicultural teacher education, like all effective education, must be developmentally appropriate. As the words of the assistant superintendent cited earlier make clear, many educators are not ready to embrace culturally sensitive, inclusive teaching. Some will concede the importance of a Black History Month or a unit on the internment of Japanese Americans in World War II, but fail to recognize their own misunderstandings, naivete, or prejudice regarding the role of cultural and racial differences in educating all students for excellence in a democratic society. Therefore, preservice teacher education programs must be sensitive to such issues as student motivation to learn, their prior knowledge about diversity and inclusive practices, differences in their learning styles, and differences in the cultural values they bring to class. Teacher education fails when it puts on ideological blinders and enacts a curriculum that focuses on the ignorance, guilt, or moral failure of students.

The goal of what follows is to present guidelines for teacher education that support the development of cross-cultural competency and inclusive teaching practices. This is done in the context of a spectrum of possible starting points for students, recognizing the developmental nature of the transformative learning involved. Three philosophical frameworks within which to consider multicultural education are presented: conservative, liberal, and critical, providing brief examples of what these frameworks might look like in schools. Each framework describes an approach that can presently be found in the schools to a greater or lesser degree. Banks' (1994) taxonomy of specific models with their connections to the three frameworks is then presented, along with suggestions for how instructors of preservice teachers can use these frameworks to encourage their students to, first, better understand and critically examine their own philosophy, and, second, consider how the specific models of curriculum and pedagogy can guide their decision making in teaching multiculturalism. The goal is transformative learning for preservice teachers—a prerequisite for the realization of Banks' goal. Finally, the various components of teacher education programs are discussed in relation to these philosophical positions and specific educational models.

It needs to be noted at the outset that multicultural education is not considered here to be a specific program that teachers implement. Nor is it conceived as a circumscribed curriculum unit or a series of events that celebrate the contributions of minority groups to American life, although these conceptions are quite common in the schools, as seen in some of the models presented below, representing as they do both conservative and liberal approaches to what is often seen as a "topic" to be "covered." Instead, multicultural education is viewed as a process of teacher–student interaction that not only respects the values of diversity but also incorporates those values into the learning of the classroom so that it may be richer, more thoughtful, and more understanding of different perspectives and life experiences. This approach to multicultural education makes use of curriculum designs and materials, of course, but is not limited to programmatic issues and definitions.

THREE FRAMEWORKS FOR MULTICULTURAL EDUCATION

The literature on multicultural education generally divides itself into three theoretical frameworks: conservative, liberal, and critical (McLaren, 1997; Webster, 1997). Each is discussed with examples from the work of Grant and Sleeter (1997).

Conservative Multiculturalism

Conservative multiculturalists assume that the conditions for justice already exist and need only be evenly apportioned. Laws such as those for equal opportunity are created to assure that social and cultural life live up to constitutional and democratic principles. Schools assimilate students into the mainstream culture and its attending values, mores, and norms. Conservative multiculturalists ignore the importance of difference in favor of an ideology of cultural homogeneity. While frequently using such language as *success for all, inclusion, empowerment,* and *equity,* they do so within the context of an assumed assimilatory educational process in which differences are expected to largely melt away and, therefore, in which specific cultures are often ignored and not included (Kozol, 1991).

Although conservative multiculturalists purport to support the goals this language represents, they believe such ends are attained in an open, free, and competitive market economy where minority groups simply have to "pull themselves up by their bootstraps." A conservative multicultural agenda in education can be summarized with the following questions that support the paradigm: How do we Americanize immigrants (bring them into the mainstream culture)? How do we prepare immigrants for a competitive economy? How do we standardize curriculum so as to give opportunities for all to compete openly for goods and services?

Clearly, a conservative multiculturalism has ideological roots in a market logic, one that tends to bypass the complex issue of cultural inclusionary practices. The goals of excellence and equity in education are then predicated on student participation in a free market of competition, opportunity, survival of the fittest, and upward social mobility. Predictors of success are primarily statistical, comparative measures, such as grades and SAT scores—the ultimate logic constructed by an ideology that places heavy emphasis on social control and competition (Kanpol, 1994). The conservative agenda includes a commitment to the same academic standards for all students and the belief that cultural differences need not play a significant role in their achievement.

Grant and Sleeter (1997) provided the label *culturally different* for the conservative approach to multiculturalism. Social mobility leading to equality comes from assimilation that requires the elimination of certain differences or deficits in knowledge, skills, and values that are barriers to the acquisition of better paying jobs. The teacher's job is to bridge the "gaps" that exist between the mainstream culture and that of the culturally different through remedial education that inculcates mainstream American knowhow. This includes attending to differences in learning styles, making connections to home and community, and identifying differences in skill levels and language proficiency. Differences are recognized with the intent of establishing pride and helping minority students understand what the mainstream culture expects and thereby to learn to conform to an Anglo schooling norm. Many elementary and secondary teachers support this conservative approach, believing that rapid assimilation into the mainstream culture is in the best interests of minority students. It is the position adopted by English immersion proponents who are opposed to bilingual programs.

One might argue that conservative multiculturalism is a contradiction in terms, especially because its goal is a kind of melting pot "uniculturalism." Nevertheless, as is seen here in the work of Banks (1994), conservative multiculturalists often recognize cultural, racial, and social differences in the context of their "contributions" to American society, although the latter are considered marginal with little impact on social and political institutions.

Liberal Multiculturalism

The liberal approach to multicultural education accents the need for diversity and cultural pluralism and the acceptance and celebration of difference. Equity and excellence are achieved through acceptance, tolerance, and understanding (Banks, 1994). Although humanistic and progressive in intent, this approach nevertheless masks the conflicts and contradictions inherent in our society, ignoring what at times seem like irreconcilable and divisive identity issues revolving around race, class, and ethnicity. Moreover, insufficient consideration is given to power constructs, control issues, and "official" knowledge, which stand in the way of achieving equity and excellence by denying political power. Rather than these barriers to equality of opportunity being dealt with as part of a potentially transformative curriculum, the emphasis is primarily on a humanistic affirmation of democratic ideals and the naïve belief that a curriculum committed to such ideals will bring about change.

Indeed, associations such as the National Association for Multicultural Education (NAME), although progressive in intent, still view equity and excellence from the vantage point of a "feel good" approach in which diversity is achieved through a humanistic agenda that promotes tolerance and acceptance but pays little attention to the role of the dominant culture in preventing equality and excellence for all.

The liberal perspective in education is most apparent in curriculum content such as Black History Month, teaching units that study, for example, the Japanese internment during World War II, and celebrations of different world cultures. Focus on cultural differences, repression, and struggle against great odds typifies the liberal approach, complemented by the celebration of the uniqueness of individual cultures. Like the conservative approach, liberal multiculturalists assume that laws and policy decisions will bring about excellence and equity within the dominant culture and free market economy. By failing to take what may be confrontational political action, liberal multiculturalists remain supportive of the dominant culture and its hegemonic power, even while, unlike conservatives, their liberalism compels them to celebrate differences to the extent that they champion equal opportunity and reject the "melting pot" concept.

Grant and Sleeter described a *human relations* approach to multiculturalism for schools that attempts to promote acceptance of diversity through intergroup education based on the sharing of feelings and values—a liberal agenda based on the goal of culturally different students living together harmoniously. Different groups are studied with the intent of establishing acceptance, mutual respect, and friendships among their members. Curriculum emphasizes stereotyping, name-calling, and cooperative learning activities and projects. A school might, for example, mobilize students and the community in food donation projects. Grant and Sleeter pointed out how this liberal approach unfortunately includes a limited analysis of why inequities exist in the first place, as well as simplistic conceptions of culture and identity. An approach focused on "let's get to know each other better" sidesteps, or is ignorant of, the root causes of racism and inequality.

Critical Multiculturalism

The critical multiculturalist believes that issues of equity and excellence cannot be effectively addressed without posing difficult but essential questions: Under what conditions and by whom are concepts of equity and excellence constructed? What do they look like for different groups and in different circumstances? Can all groups benefit equally from a particular construction of these concepts? What happens when different groups and individuals view these concepts differently? How can equity and excellence be achieved in a society in which historically the dominant culture has determined their meaning? The critical approach seeks justice by focusing on the relationships between equity and excellence, on one hand, and race, ethnic, and class configurations, on the other hand. It believes that leaving these matters to the processes of free market competition and upward social mobility will only deny the achievement of justice.

For the critical multiculturalist, knowledge is not value free, but shaped culturally, historically, ethnically, and linguistically. In Giroux's (1988) words, knowledge "never speaks for itself, but rather is constantly mediated through the ideoiogical and cultural experiences that students bring to the classroom" (p. 100). Put another way, "the act of knowing is integrally related to the power of self-definition" (Giroux, 1995, p. 133). Therefore, the histories and narratives of subordinate groups must be a part of the school curriculum if their members are to engage in personally meaningful learning and if equity and excellence are to be properly served. Curriculum must be transformative, and educators as critical multiculturalists must enter into a democratic dialogue with each other to develop programs that promote critical reflection and inclusionary knowledge.

Critical multiculturalists believe that schools impose standards on children that reinforce the power relationships and social stratification of American society. Curriculum policy, for example, is usually committed to White, middle-class values that deny to the powerless and disenfranchised equal access to knowledge. When those in power determine educational policy, whether they be professional commissions, governmental agencies, or school district authorities, the result, argues the critical multiculturalist, is a standardization around content that effectively excludes the voices and experiences of those not in power. A not-so-hidden curriculum is created that reflects the social inequalities of the society the schools serve, despite cultural celebrations of difference sponsored by liberal educators.

Grant and Sleeter (1997) presented three models of multiculturalism for schools that, taken in order, become increasingly critical in their structure: *single group studies, cultural pluralism,* and *social reconstructionist.* The first of these focuses on one group at a time and seeks to explain why a particular group has experienced discrimination within society. With the goal of increasing the status of the group, single group studies endorses education that develops a critical consciousness in students regarding the need for change for the identified group. The classroom would include displays reflecting the culture and contributions of the group, and speakers from the group would be invited to address the class to "tell their story." Important distinctions are made among groups, for example, Asians are not lumped together but are considered separately—clearly, Cambodians and Laotians do not share the same history as Chinese and Japanese. Superficial similarities are put aside in favor of significant distinctions.

The second model, cultural pluralism, embraces, as its name suggests, cultural pluralism and social equality in society and the schools. The metaphors of "tossed salad" or "mosaic" replace "melting pot," and the curriculum examines the perspectives and contributions of several different groups. Rather than being limited to the study of particular minority groups, the goal is to reduce prejudice by helping students adapt to as much diversity as possible and to learn the importance of power equity and social justice for all groups. Rejecting a dominant Anglo mainstream, the goal is equitable power distribution in the school as well as the society. As a form of critical multiculturalism, it is more inclusive in its focus than targeting just a single group study, even though the latter may attempt to cover many groups over the course of several years of study.

The social reconstructivist approach is the most visionary and critical of the Grant and Sleeter's models. It directly challenges students to become social reformers and commit to the reconstruction of society through the redistribution of power and other resources. The curriculum teaches social action skills, promotes cultural pluralism and alternative lifestyles, and has students analyze oppression with the intent of eventually, if not immediately, taking action to work for a more democratic society. Unlike the liberal human relations approach, which focuses on how individuals can get along with each other, social reconstructivism promotes ways in which groups can change structures. In this regard, community action projects are important and active learning takes center stage.

BANKS' MODELS OF MULTICULTURAL CURRICULUM AND PEDAGOGY

In order to better understand of how the three theoretical frameworks just discussed—conservative, liberal, and critical—can be useful to the schools, the multicultural curriculum and pedagogy models of Banks (1994) are extremely useful. They demonstrate how elements of all three frameworks can work both alone and in combination to move schools toward a curriculum characterized by both equity and excellence. As such, they complement the models of Grant and Sleeter briefly described.

Banks labels his four approaches *contributions, additive, transformative,* and *social action.* Each reflects one or more of the three philosophical frameworks. Taken together, they offer a variety of approaches—several eclectic—for moving schools toward an approach to multiculturalism that is transformative in its inclusion of the voices and experiences of all students. The options provided allow for a developmental approach that recognizes that changes in attitude and approach to teaching come only after much critical self-reflection that shapes new mental schema and attitudes. How these options might be incorporated into a teacher education program is discussed next.

Contributions

As the name suggests, the contributions approach to multicultural education emphasizes what minority groups have contributed to society. As such, it includes elements of both the conservative and liberal frameworks. The dominant culture recognizes the special qualities of diversity that have made America richer and more interesting. Black History Month, International Food Day, the study of ethnic festivals and the heroes of different cultures are included in a curriculum that otherwise and primarily is devoted to the contributions of Western White males to the dominant culture. Conservatives who support this approach will argue that there is representation in the curriculum of most minority groups and that students are therefore learning about other cultures.

To those who question the commitment of this approach to multicultural education, implementers will point to specific places in the curriculum where attention is paid to minority groups. They might say, for example, "We have a world cultures course," or "We teach a unit on the American Indians that avoids stereotyping," or "We have an American history unit that includes the contributions of women." The argument is that the school has accommodated the study of ethnic, racial, and gender differences.

The contributions approach attempts to sensitize the majority White culture to some understanding of minority groups' history as a part of the American experience. However, without an accompanying active change agenda, it may in fact support Grant and Sleeter's conservative culturally different model and its goal of a melting pot, homogeneous culture. The contributions model often settles for a kind of cosmetic multiculturalism—one that allows administrators and teachers to say, "We've taken care of that issue" when questioned, for example, by activist community groups. In its feel good and humanistic approach it does have liberal qualities; unfortunately, many schools never get beyond it to a study of the issues of power and disenfranchisement.

Additive

Once again, the name suggests this model's approach to multiculturalism. Additive refers to the adding on of multicultural material in order to address what has been heretofore ignored. For example, an English teacher may decide to teach Alice Walker's *The Color Purple* in addition to the tradition-al Western literary canon because she believes that the African-American experience, as represented in fiction, has been unfairly ignored. This approach shares both conservative and liberal elements: conservative when its importance is viewed primarily as a perfunctory gesture toward fairness; liberal when its importance is viewed as a substantive addition to a study of the diversity of the American experience and when sufficient curricular time is devoted to doing so.

Additive suggests that there is more to teach, not less. The danger is that if the material becomes an official part of the curriculum, it may be given short shrift—or not taught at all—by teachers who fail to accept its impor-tance, thinly disguising their feelings by claiming that there is not enough time in the year to teach everything required. Part of the conservatism of the additive approach may be, then, the potential unwillingness of the school or department to make the teaching manageable if not inviting by providing adequate space in the curriculum to give the new material its due. In such instances, the text or unit may easily remain of lesser importance in the eyes of many teachers and students.

The additive model resonates with Grant and Sleeter's Human Relations and single group studies models only if it is approached seriously and sub-stantively, rather than perfunctorily. That is, if what is added becomes the basis for a serious study of human relations or the study of a particular minority group with the goal of developing greater understanding and acceptance of the group, then it contributes to the goals of these two models.

Transformative

Rather than simply adding on to the curriculum, the transformative approach requires that the internal structure of the curriculum be changed to incorporate the fabric of the racial, ethnic, and social experiences of dif-ferent minority groups. For example, a unit on the family would consider family experiences of a variety of families representing different cultures and family groupings. The study of the Civil War would consider issues of race, class and gender inequities. Units of study are constructed around different perspectives and points of view so that students learn a critical stance with respect to issues, including the values and assumptions of their own cultures. The goal is a transformation of students' perspectives regarding issues of equity and justice.

The transformative approach to multicultural education is primarily critical in its emphasis on an examination of underlying cultural assump-tions, its study of diversity in relation to the dominant culture, and in its democratic goal of educating for equity and justice. Students learn to be reflective, to adopt different perspectives, and to understand how what they are taught—the knowledge that schooling offers—has been shaped historically, ethnically, culturally, and linguistically. In its concern for dealing seriously with issues of injustice and inequality, rather than merely giving them lip service, the approach also incorporates some liberal values. However, the liberal faith in the ability of societal institutions as currently constituted to bring about substantive change sets it apart from the transformative approach.

The emphasis of the transformative approach on using diversity as a primary touchstone for the development of curriculum will alienate many teachers. In communities where minority representation or tolerance for existing diversity within the community is low, such an approach will inevitably fail. Many schools will not embrace this model until they and their communities have themselves been transformed and accept diversity as a major theme in the development of curriculum and in the teaching that occurs in the classroom.

Banks' transformative model echoes Grant and Sleeter's cultural pluralism and social reconstructionist models. All three have as their ultimate goal the transformation of society through an understanding of how knowledge and power operate in society and through learning to work to bring about social justice. Differences are more a matter of degree: Grant and Sleeter's cultural pluralism and Banks' transformative model involves less of an action-oriented approach in their efforts to work for tolerance, acceptance, and equity than does Grant and Sleeter's social reconstructionist model or—as is seen here—Banks' social action approach.

Social Action

Social action is an extension of the transformative approach and echoes. Rather than merely studying the issues through a restructured curriculum, social action calls for student action to deal with injustice and inequity. Students carry out research/action projects, and they suggest ways that change can be initiated. Through their work, they see how the dominant culture perpetuates inequality and how even they are responsible for supporting oppressive institutions. Most importantly, teachers encourage students to be heard on local diversity issues and to become actively involved in groups that work for change. One learns by doing, and until the learner becomes actively involved in the issues, knowledge remains largely inert and impotent, and how it is constructed is at best only dimly understood. Community-based learning is becoming a more popular curriculum component; the social action model views such learning as a tool for implementing critical skills to bring about change.

In its commitment to working for transformative change in local communities, social action is a form of critical multiculturalism. Many liberals would fail to endorse the model because of its direct confrontation of hegemonic institutions as instruments of oppression and guardians of the status quo. Although liberal multiculturalists endorse curriculum projects whose goals are increased tolerance and understanding of minority groups, many would not support student projects that seriously question the commitments of social institutions to principles of democracy and that call for students to directly confront and challenge such institutions.

Nor would many middle-class communities support the social action model. Individual teachers in the past have been persecuted if not fired for taking what are viewed as radical positions regarding issues of social justice and equity. However, projects that bring students together with community leaders who recognize the need for change, even when these leaders reflect a liberal belief in the basic worth or integrity of the institutions they represent, can be productive of a truly transformative education.

Social action is very similar to Grant and Sleeter's social reconstructivist model in its emphasis on developing the commitment and critical skills to take action for the cause of social justice. Both models address oppression and social inequality with the aim of reconstructing society to better serve democratic aims.

IMPLICATIONS FOR TEACHER EDUCATION: THE NEED FOR TRANSFORMATIVE LEARNING

As noted in the introduction, the primarily White and middle-class teachers in our nation's schools are ill prepared in knowledge, skills, and attitude to teach for equity and excellence in multicultural classrooms. They cannot teach for cross-cultural competency when they lack it themselves. Teacher education programs intent on changing this situation must recognize the necessity of providing learning experiences that increase the likelihood that preservice teachers will undergo transformative learning regarding multicultural education.

Prospective teachers must be critically reflective regarding their own philosophical position, moral commitment, and readiness to teach for equity and excellence if they are to develop cross-cultural competency. For this reason, the curriculum for preservice teachers must include confronting the relative strengths and weaknesses of the philosophical frameworks and specific multicultural models just presented. Through self-reflection triggered by the study of perspectives that challenge preconceived assumptions significant changes in beliefs, attitudes, and knowledge can occur.

Preservice teachers can locate their own current views of multicultural education at some point on the spectrum of conservative to critical philosophical frameworks and models. Questions to consider are these: Which of these models best represents the experience of multicultural education that I encountered in my schooling? What is my current philosophy regarding multicultural education and what are its implications for my teaching? Do any of the models challenge me to critically examine my current position and my conception of pedagogy for teaching students who differ racially, culturally, and socially? What do I need to learn in order to better prepare myself to teach in multicultural classrooms? The considerations that these questions entail are explored here as part of the discussion of how the philosophical frameworks and teaching models previously discussed can be incorporated into the curriculum of preservice education.

Preservice teachers with little multicultural experience need to acquire the appropriate knowledge and skills, but they also must reconceive their role as teachers by recognizing the primary importance of diversity in all of their educational decision making, from determining student readiness for learning, to designing curricula, selecting instructional materials, assessing performance, and developing appropriate programs and teaching techniques. Approaching teaching in this way is very different than assuming that a context-neutral, mainstream pedagogy and curriculum are appropriate for all students. It is an approach that is very much grounded in Banks' transformative models and Grant and Sleeter's cultural pluralism.

When preservice teachers study these models presented, they will assess the strengths and weaknesses of each based on their own philosophical position regarding multiculturalism. To suggest that ideally the instructor's goal is to move students toward a critical philosophical framework is, of course, to reveal our biases regarding what approach best serves teaching for a just and democratic society. Whether preservice teachers change their beliefs depends on the impact that preservice education has on their prior knowledge and attitudes. Highly ideological approaches that strongly favor a critical philosophy will often meet with resistance. Nevertheless, by having preservice teachers consider the teaching and learning implications of such models as, on the one hand, the culturally different and contributions models—primarily conservative approaches—and, on the other hand, the reconstructivist and social action models—primarily critical approaches, preservice teachers will better understand the choices available and can critically examine their own viewpoints and those of the schools in which they will teach.

The importance of student teachers studying these different models is underscored by the prevalence of assimilationist, human relations, and additive models of multicultural education in teacher education curricula (Sleeter, 1994; Sleeter & Grant, 1994). Little change in student teachers' conceptualizations of and attitudes toward multicultural education can be expected to occur if these dominant models are not contrasted with more philosophically critical ones. As Yeo (1997a) explains,

> new teachers must develop a critical understanding of the intricate and profound complexion of race, ethnicity, ideology, gender, ethics, and similar issues that schools and teachers of education neglect to address . . . unfortunately, all too often, teacher education has chosen to reinforce rather than challenge. (pp. 140-141)

Teacher education programs must also include field experiences in urban settings in which students directly observe the need for multicultural education and pedagogy in schools with diverse student populations. For many White and middle-class college students this is a new experience—one that forces them to seriously consider whether the learning needs of all students are being appropriately served and how to adapt the content of instruction and teaching style to students' cultural and individual learning preferences. Assignments in courses that accompany field experiences should focus on these issues so that theory and practice are interrelated. Field experiences will confront preservice teachers with concrete examples of the multicultural models just presented, making them real and compelling and revealing their relative effectiveness in serving the goals of equity and excellence. Students who have had a variety of field experiences often report amazement at the culturally insensitive attitudes of some teachers—even, at times, minority teachers, who advocate the culturally different model and teach to remediate "deficiencies," or who support the contributions model, in which minority cultures are only occasionally celebrated.

Pedagogy courses should also require students to work closely with individual minority students in tutorial relationships in order that they may gain a more sensitive and concrete understanding of how culture shapes learning styles and of the importance of giving all students more choices about how they will learn. The strengths and weaknesses of the different curriculum and pedagogical models will become more apparent as preservice teachers begin to understand the learning needs of individual minority students.

Preservice courses should also include experience with Banks' transformative approach to multiculturalism by assisting preservice teachers in developing teaching units that educate students about minority groups, racist views, and the inequities of political and social institutions. They can explore ways that units of this kind can be integrated into a school's social studies curriculum and monitor their own comfort level in doing such work. For some preservice teachers, this task may not be a comfortable one, especially if they support a less critical approach to multiculturalism, but through such immersion in curriculum planning and hopefully the eventual teaching of the unit in field experience settings or student teaching itself, students reflect on their own values and pedagogical stance. They should also discuss how different schools in different settings might accept such a critically based unit—whether, for example, students and the community in predominantly Anglo communities would label it biased, too radical, and unacceptably critical of majority views and institutions.

Prospective teachers should also become knowledgeable regarding curriculum publications that can assist them in teaching multicultural issues. For example, Teaching Tolerance, a project of the Southern Poverty Law Center, is an example of a program designed to help teachers become more effective in addressing intolerance and racism. Included are teaching units such as The American Civil Rights Movement and The Shadow of Hate, along with a *Teaching Tolerance* magazine. Most importantly, it includes training in the teaching of tolerance. An important activity would be to have students determine which of the multicultural models programs of this kind support, analyzing them for their strengths and weaknesses.

By designing their own units and evaluating prepackaged programs, teacher education students will become more skilled in making judgments about effective curriculum and pedagogy. The philosophical frameworks and specific teaching models can serve as useful lenses through which to both design and evaluate teaching materials and instructional techniques.

Students should also gain practice using highly interactive instruction that appeal to many learning styles, such as heterogeneous grouping, cooperative learning, discovery learning, and peer tutoring. These methods need to be considered in relation to culture-specific contexts, not merely as generic methods that can be equally successful with all students. In their sensitivity to the needs of particular groups, they support liberal and critical approaches to multicultural education. Micro-teaching is a useful format, and students should be required to demonstrate how what they are teaching addresses the needs of diverse students. Along with the experiences just discussed, such pedagogy should be infused throughout the teacher education curriculum, particularly in field experiences and student teaching, rather than being dealt with through an additive approach that merely appends it to existing courses or packs it into one required course that purports to deal with all of multicultural education.

Multicultural infusion is a key component of a teacher education program that aims for transfomative learning. Cross-cultural competency is not developed in any one course or in an academic vacuum. It depends on students having cultural knowledge, direct intercultural experiences, and the opportunity to reflect on those experiences. It is both personal and interpersonal, cognitive and affective. For this reason, a multicultural program for preservice teachers must not be limited to the education department or school of education. The larger college or university is able to provide speakers, campus organizations, and community projects that present opportunities for cross-cultural communication and a sharing of opinions that promote cultural pluralism and transformative educational models. Departments can incorporate a multicultural perspective into many of their courses and include a social justice component that, by making connections between course concepts and experiential learning in the community outside of the institution, takes a reconstructivist or social action approach to multicultural education. If social justice is a part of the university's mission, projects that provide direct experience with social justice issues should appear throughout the university, not only as components of education courses.

The capstone of the preservice experience, student teaching, provides the opportunity for supervisors to focus on multicultural issues as they confront the student teacher in real time. But as noted earlier, supervisors instead usually concentrate on helping students assimilate into school cultures that are all too often characterized by the contributions or additive approach to these issues. While it may be difficult to deal with global multicultural themes during student teaching when the survival mode takes over and the time is short, as Abt-Perkins et al. (2000) pointed out, supervisors can highlight the importance of how cultural, social, and ethnic factors impact the learning of individual students by conferencing with their student teachers regarding the short-term benefits of considering these factors in terms of their relationships with their students. These researchers discovered that in postobservation conferences instructional concerns could be framed along cultural dimensions:

> In dialogue during post observation conferences, we shared our cultural framing and reframing of our observation of the lesson, opening possibilities for interpretation of various instructional choices and helping us to discuss the cultural consequences of instructional decisions. Modeling this type of reflection with our student teachers encouraged them to raise cultural questions about their own practices. (pp. 45-46)

If the field supervisor is also knowledgeable about the philosophical frameworks and curriculum and pedagogical models just presented, he or she can help the student teacher make connections between them and such specific classroom matters as lesson planning and minute-by-minute instructional decisions, resulting in the merging of theory and practice in ways that support cognitive dissonance and the recognition of the inadequacy of teaching from assimilative, additive, or "contributions" models of curriculum and pedagogy.

It is particularly important that instructors of preservice courses undergo transformative learning in their own understanding of and commitment to more liberal and critical models of curriculum and pedagogy for multicultural education. Cochran-Smith (2000) discussed just such a transformation in her own instruction that resulted from rather dramatic self-revelations concerning the inadequacy of her approach to the subject of racism—an approach that she had assumed addressed the topic significantly and meaningfully through much philosophically critical reading and in-class discussion of the issues. She warned against courses that privilege pedagogy drawn from the theories and practices developed primarily by White teachers and scholars of child development, language learning, and progressive education. Ironically, she comes to realize that the subtle message of her course had been that progressive pedagogy was culture neutral, even though she had been emphasizing through a critical approach that all aspects of schooling were socially and culturally constructed.

Cochran-Smith recommended the inclusion of theories of practice developed by and about people of color, along with "rich and detailed analyses of successful teachers of urban children, particularly poor children of color, who use a variety of pedagogies" (p. 179). Her own transformative learning includes becoming convinced that "reading and writing accounts about race and racism that get personal, as well as reading more intellectualized arguments about these issues, is vital to preservice teacher education" (p. 173). These include the narratives of her own students. When the preservice curriculum is viewed critically as "racial text," transformative learning is encouraged, for racism becomes a central issue in the course and is dealt with on close and personal levels, not just through "distant and academic" prose. Moreover, such a curriculum, evolving out of a critical philosophy, involves helping students understand that schools are always "sites for institutional and collective struggles of power and oppression, not neutral backdrops for individual achievement and failure" (p. 174).

In her inclusion of the narratives of minority teachers and students, as well as the theories of the dominant professional educational culture, Cochran-Smith's curriculum has evolved in a manner that demonstrates that the knowledge we have about effective teaching is socially and culturally constructed and therefore context dependent, rather than a set of uniform prescriptions that can ignore racial, ethnic, and social differences. Additionally, by involving preservice teachers in their own construction of such knowledge, her pedagogy increases the likelihood of their experiencing transformative learning regarding equity and excellence in schools, including the recognition of the importance of using critical multicultural approaches in curriculum development and teaching practices.

Cochran-Smith's course underscores the importance of a critical approach to teacher education. Because of the three philosophical positions presented previously, it has the greatest potential for transforming understanding and attitudes. For example, when students recognize that the work of professional educational theorists is itself culturally constructed knowledge, they are in a better position to accept the legitimacy of the cultural knowledge of minority students. Also, they are usually compelled to critically assess their own mental "constructions" or schema of what constitute authoritative and perceptive accounts of the lives of minority students and the curriculum and pedagogy that is most appropriate for them. Cochran-Smith provided a potentially powerful critical approach that speaks to the transformative and cultural pluralism models, pointing the way to social reconstructivist and social action positions and eventual cross-cultural competency.

Once the student teacher is out in the schools, he or she may have little opportunity to continue to experience transformative learning regarding the teaching of minority students unless the school leadership provides opportunities through ongoing multicultural professional development efforts. For this reason, the importance of experiential as well as academic course work during preservice teacher education is underscored if students are to make a career-long commitment to becoming cross-culturally competent. Students need the field and student teaching experiences, the one-on-one work with minority students, and the experience with social justice projects in order for the study of multiculturalism to touch their emotional and moral lives and, therefore, to engender a commitment to life-long transformative learning that when necessary challenges the norms and values of the schools in which they will spend their careers.

CONCLUSION

The philosophical frameworks and specific multicultural models presented here are best used as interpretive lenses through which students can critically examine their own positions and the manner in which they organize their teaching to support multicultural education. Moreover, perceptive students who understand that the models themselves are culturally constructed are likely to develop a critical, self-reflective stance regarding the values that define them, which, in turn, will encourage their own transformative learning. Recognizing the politics of inclusion in relation to multicultural education supports the critical awareness necessary for transformative understanding, or what Cranton (1996) referred to as "emancipatory knowledge" (p. 20).

Students can move back and forth between the academic and the experiential in a preservice program that includes course work infused with multicultural issues, multicultural experiences within the total university community, and fieldwork and student teaching that include working with minority students. In this way, preservice students are immersed in a learning environment that supports the development of cross-cultural competency and an inclusive curriculum and pedagogy committed to equity and excellence for all students.

REFERENCES

Apt-Perkins, D., Hauschildt, P., & Dale, H. (2000). Becoming multicultural supervisors: Lessons from a collaborative field study. *Journal of Curriculum and Supervision, 16*(1), 28-47.

Banks, J. (1994). *An introduction to multicultural education.* Boston: Allyn & Bacon.

Britzman, D. (1991). Practice makes practice. Albany: State University of New York Press.

Cochran-Smith, M. (2000). Blind vision: Unlearning racism in teacher education. *Harvard Educational Review, 70*(2), 157-190.

Cranton, P. (1996). *Professional development as transformative learning.* San Francisco: Jossey-Bass.

Cuban, L. (1984). *How teachers taught, constancy and change in American classrooms.* New York: Longman.

Darder, A. (1991). *Culture and power in the classroom—A critical foundation for bicultural education.* New York: Begin & Garvey.

Everhart, R. (1983). *Reading, writing, and resistance—Adolescence and labor in junior high school.* Boston: Routledge & Kegan.

Feiman-Nemser, S., & Buchmann, M. (1985). Pitfalls of experience in teacher education. *Teachers College Record, 87*, 53-66.

Giroux, H. (1988). *Teachers as intellectuals: Toward a critical pedagogy of learning.* Granby, MA: Bergin and Garvey.

Giroux, H. (1995). Teaching in the age of political correctness. *The Education Forum.* (Kappa Delta Pi), *59*, 130-139.

Goodlad, J. (1984). *A place called school: Prospects for the future.* New York: McGraw Hill.

Grant, C., & Sleeter, C. (1987). Multicultural education. *Harvard Educational Review, 57* (4), 421-444.

Grant, C. & Sleeter, C. (1994). *Making choices for multicultural education: Five approaches to race, class, and gender* (2nd ed.). New York: Macmillan.

Grant, C., & Sleeter, C. (1997). *Turning on learning* (2nd ed.). Upper Saddle River, NJ: Merrill-Prentice-Hall.

Kanpol, B. (1994). *Critical pedagogy: An introduction.* Westport, CT: Bergin & Garvey.

Kanpol, B., & McLaren, P. (1995). *Critical multiculturalism: Uncommon voices in a common struggle.* Westport, CT: Bergin & Garvey.

King, J. (1991). Dysconscious racism: Ideology, identity, and the miseducation of teachers. *Journal of Negro Education*, 133-146.

Kozol, J. (1991). *Savage inequalities.* New York: Crown.

Kozol, J. (1994). *Amazing grace.* New York: Crown.

LaBelle, T.J. (1976). An anthropological framework for studying education. In J.I. Roberts & S.K. Akinsanya (Eds.), *Educational patterns and cultural configurations: The anthropology of education.* New York: David McKay.

Ladson-Billings, G. (2000). Preparing teachers for diversity: Historical perspectives, current trends, and future directions. In L. Darling-Hammond & G. Sykes (Eds.), *Teaching as the learning profession: Handbook of policy and practice.* San Francisco: Jossey-Bass.

McLaren, P. (1997). *Revolutionary multiculturalism.* Boulder CO: Westview Press.

Nieto, S. (1996). *Affirming diversity: The sociopolitical context of multicultural education.* New York: Longman.

Richardson-Koehler, V. (1988). Barriers to the effective supervision of student teaching: A field study. *Journal of Teacher Education, 39*(2), 28-34.

Sleeter, C. (1992). Restructuring schools for multicultural education. *Journal of Teacher Education, 43*, 141-148.

Sleeter, C. (1994). *Multicultural education, social positionality and whiteness.* Paper presented at annual meeting of the American Educational Research Association, New Orleans.

Webster, Y. (1997). *Against the multicultural agenda: A critical thinking approach.* Westport, CT: Praeger.

Yeo, F. (1997a). Teacher preparation and inner-city schools: Sustaining educational failure. *The Urban Review, 29*(2), 127-143.

Zeichner, K., & Hoeft, K. (1996). Teacher socialization for cultural diversity. In J. Sikula, T. J. Buttery, & E. Guyton (Ed.), *Handbook of research on teacher education.* New York: Macmillan.

5

Curriculum and Inclusion

An Interdisciplinary Platform
of Possibility

Barry Kanpol

Indiana University-Purdue University Fort Wayne

Many of the previous chapters have alluded both overtly and covertly to the issues of curriculum and inclusion, as well as to their theoretical constructs. Clearly, there is no one correct method to instill our students with the correct "how to's" regarding inclusion, particularly as many students have learned that *inclusion* is often a confusing term with multiple meanings. Nevertheless, I feel, as I know others do in this volume, that talking about the politics of inclusion or the inclusion of politics would and could not suffice without an attempt to include student voices into the "picture" as to how curriculum speaks to the issues we have been discussing.

With these former students I built a 3-week unit plan formed around the themes embraced by an inclusionary politics. On an macro-level, this is a unit that incorporates the multicultural issues and trends discussed by Lee in chapter 5, the "voice" issues discussed by Applegate in chapter 4, and curriculum integration issues delivered by Brady in chapter 1. On a micro-level, this is a unit attempted by myself and my students to connect these themes to the practical issues of creating a more inclusive and democratic environment for students. My hope is that our pre- and in-service teachers can read the unit and garner meaning that can be adopted as they proceed into their professional lives as teachers. My sincere thanks to these five students who supported me in the writing of this unit plan: Jill Deimler, Jaci Keagy, Tanya Kissell, Michele Graham Newbury, and Angela Ryan.

UNIT PLAN

Theme: Similarities within Differences through Multiculturalism

Theme Description: The unit will attempt to uncover, explore, and critique the multiple identifies of students, their similarities and differences, and the stereotypes prevalent within these cultures. Within trying to foster an acceptance of difference and similarities of these cultures (Asiasn, Hispanic, African American, and European American), literature, drama, and the fine arts will be the major content areas. The structure of the unit looks like this:

Similarities within Differences
Through Multiculturalism
In
Literature
Drama
Fine Arts
With
Asian American
Hispanic
African American and
European American Cultures

This unit can be used anywhere from Grades 7 and 9 onward; levels of materials would have to be modified or enhanced depending on the class make-up, class size, and age level.

Unit Length

This is a 3-month unit.

Major Goals

1. To break the cycle of stereotypical thinking and cultural prejudice and to demonstrate the similarities within our differences of various cultures.
2. For students to find their own cultural voices so they can begin to empathize with others.

Major Objectives

1. Students will learn to critique themselves.
2. Through self-critique, students will learn to appreciate the worth and dignity of others.
3. Students will empathize with and respect the contributions of the Asian, Hispanic, African-American, and European American cultures as they contribute to the richness of their personal culture and our national culture.
4. Students will learn about differences as they relate to their own lives and others' lives.

Class Make-Up

The class is made up of 30 students in Grade 10: 20 females and 10 males. Race: 18 white, 6 African American, 3 Hispanic and 3 Asian. Socioeconomic status: working-class school in working-class industrial neighborhood.

Monthly Objectives

First Month

1. Through the vehicle of literature, students will compare values and attitudes of the four cultures selected for learning.
2. Students will explore how literature simulates the lived experiences of different cultures.
3. Students will recognize the validity of multiple realities.
4. Through literary examples, students will attempt to overcome stereotypical cultural judgments and prejudices.

Second Month

Same objectives as for the first month, except that drama will be the medium for exploration.

Third Month

Same as for the first month, except that music and art will be the medium for exploration.

Each month has four objectives. Each objective relates to at least one week's lessons. Thus, there would be 12 to 14 weeks to this unit. However, flexibility is needed so that anyone attempting such a unit will realize that these objectives are intertwined and may overlap at times. The following lesson plans and weekly and daily objectives are exemplars and suggestions that can be used in such a critical pedagogy unit. These lesson plans are not correct or perfect! They have been created to be critiqued.

Weekly Objectives, Week 1

Lesson Plan Outline Week 1, Day 1

Daily Objective 1.   Students will assess their own level of competence in dealing with cross-cultural education and multicultural awareness.

Procedure.   Individual activity. Students receive self-assessment sheet (to be prepared individually by teachers). Students will place each of the terms on the appropriate place in the continuum based on their self-assessment. These sheets will be collected and placed in each student's portfolio.

Sources

Adapted from *Multicltural Education: A Cross Cultural Training Approach.* Yarmouth, MA: Intercultural Press.

Daily Objective 2.   Students will determine how we select what we see, and how one's background and attitudes could impact on a perception of an object or an event.

Procedure.   Multiple-level picture interpretations are shown in the class for 10 seconds (each teacher to choose picture). Each student writes what he or she saw. Students share responses with a partner. Volunteers demonstrate through dialogue different interpretations of pictures. Follow-up discussion in groups of three or four using cooperative learning techniques.

Questions for Discussion (in groups of three or four).

1. How do we select out of our perception the things we want to see?
2. Why is it sometimes difficult to see things that are obviously there?
3. How does our attitude influence our perception?
4. How can we open our minds to see things that we may not have been seen before?

Note: This discussion should be allowed to continue for as long as it needs to accommodate all cultural voices.

Materials. Photographs, pictures, transparency, overhead projector, cards with discussion questions (one card per group).

Assignment. Students write a one-page autobiography.

Lesson Plan Outline Week 1, Day 2

Daily Objective 1. Students will attempt to learn to praise themselves and increase their self-esteem.

Procedure. Using the cooperative learning technique think–pair–share, students are asked to think of:

1. Two physical attributes about themselves that they like.
2. Two personality qualities that they like.
3. One talent or skill that they possess.

After completing think–pair–share, a follow-up discussion in class will focus on these questions:

1. Did you find this a difficulty assignment? Why or why not?
2. Is it more difficulty to praise yourself or someone else? Why?
3. Are more people quick to give a negative comment about themselves or others than they are to compliment them? Why or why not?

Daily Objective 2. Students will recognize the importance of individual differences and sensitivity to personal characteristics.

Procedure.

1. Distribute an orange to each student. Each student is to examine, inspect, and get to know his or her fruit. Have students name their fruit and identify strengths and weaknesses in it.
2. Collect and mix up the oranges in front of the class.
3. Students write a short autobiographical paragraph about their fruit.
4. Ask students to come forward and collect their own fruit.

Questions for Discussion (in groups of three or four.

1. How many of you are sure you claimed your original fruit? How do you know?
2. What role did skin color play in getting to know your fruit?
3. Why can't we get to know people as quickly as we got to know our oranges?

Share answers and reflections in class using the cooperative learning technique stand and share.

Materials.   One orange per student, cards with discussion questions for each group.

Assignment.   Introduction to use of student journals. These journals will be used throughout the unit to encourage students to write feelings and personal interpretations of class activities. The journals will become a part of the student evaluation.

Student journal reflection for today:

- What parallels do you see in differentiating between oranges and between people? What differences exist?
- What was important in helping you to differentiate your orange from the others?
- Personal reflection on this exercise.

Evaluation.

- Participation in discussion
- Group participation
- Completion of journal entry

Sources

Kaga, S. (1992). *Cooperative learning*. San Jan Capistrano, CA: Kagan Cooperative Learning.
Newstrom, J.W., & Scannell, E.E. (1980). *Games trainers play*. New York: McGraw-Hill.

Other Suggested Activities for Week 1–Lesson Plans to Be Prepared by Reader or User of This Text

1. Students prepare an autobiographical collage of photos, magazine pictures, fabric, and so on, anything that has meaning to them in their lives. Hold a class discussion of beliefs, backgrounds, and attitudes that help determine students' personal realities.
2. Students explore their own values and the values of other cultural groups. This can be done with value charts, ranking a list of values generated by the students, or using parables or anecdotes that illustrate different value systems.

3. Class building and community building activities should be included to facilitate group development, inclusion, trust, and respect. Numerous activities of this type are included in the following sources.

Sources

Pusch, M.D. (1979). *Multicultural education: A cross cultural approach.* Yarmouth, ME: Intercultural Press.
Shaw, V. (1992). *Community building in the classroom.* San Jan Capistrano, CA: Kagan Cooperative Learning.

Weekly Objectives, Week 2

Students will compare their own attitudes and values to those found in Asian literature. In addition, students will become aware of stereotypical judgments and their harmful effects.

Lesson Plan Outline Week 2, Day 1

Daily Objective.   Students will recognize the collective voice in the poem "We the Dangerous."

Procedure.   Students will read the poem at first to themselves. Students will then, in groups of three, take a part (I, we, they) and read the poem aloud, utilizing a choral approach.

Materials.   The poem "We the Dangerous"

Assignment.   After discussing the different identities of the I, we, and they of the poem, students will write an explanation of their voice within American society, specifying the I voice, we voice, and they voice.

Evaluation.

- Participation in choral reading
- Participation in class discussion
- Completion of voice assignment

Source

Mirikitani, J. (1991). We the dangerous. In *American mosaic: Multicultural readings in context.* Boston: Houghton Mifflin.

Sample Daily Objectives for Remainder of Week 2

1. Students will sensitize themselves to the concept of culture. They will list several ways the short story "In the Land of the Free" represents the fears and loss of culture and identity that plague many new immigrants to the United States.
2. Students will identify in a journal entryways in which their culture has lost some of its identity, either intentionally or unintentionally.
3. Students will analyze the motivation and behavior of James Clancy.
4. Students will write a poem about an experience that has affected them strongly or write a journal entry discussing the benefits of writing as an emotional outlet.

Source

Far, S.S. (1991). In the land of the free. In *American mosaic: Multicultural readings in context*. Boston: Houhton Mifflin.

Okada, J. (1991). No-no-boy. In *American mosaic: Multicultural readings in context*. Boston: Houghton Mifflin.

Weekly Objectives: Week 3

Students will compare their own attitudes and values to those found in Hispanic literature. In addition, students will become aware of stereotypical judgments and their harmful effects.

Suggested Literature Titles and Activities

Read the short story "Ropes of passage" and poems "Milagros" and "Napa, California."

Sample Daily Objectives:

1. Students will learn about the concept of alienation by naming and discussing examples of alienation from "Milagros."
2. Students will sensitize themselves to injustice by comparing the struggles and injustices Hispanic immigrants found in "Ropes of Passage" to those of American immigrants.
3. Students will identify different belief systems by understanding how incidents from "Ropes of Passage" illustrate how society's beliefs and attitudes influences Santo's life. Students will create a list of their family's beliefs and attitudes.

4. Students will analyze the correlation between the we in the poem "Napa, California' to the we in the poem "We the Dangerous."

Source

Castillo, A. (1991). Milagros. In *American mosaic: Multicultural readings in context.* (Boston: Houghton Mifflin.
Castillo, A. (1991). Napa, California. In *American mosaic: Multicultural reading in context.* Boston: Houghton Mifflin.
Rivera, E. (1991). Ropes of passage. In *American mosaic: Multicultural readings in context.* Boston: Houghton Mifflin.

Additional Optional Sources

Mohr, N. (1991). A Thanksgiving celebration. In *American mosaic: Multilcultural readings in context.* Boston: Houghton Mifflin.
Thomas, Piri. "Puerto Rican paradise." Colon, Jesus. "Stowaway."

Weekly Objectives, Week 4

Students will compare their own attitudes and values to those found in African-American literature. In addition, students will become aware of stereotypical judgments and their harmful effects.

Suggested Literature Titles and Activities

- View the video of Martin Luther King, Jr.'s speech "I Have a Dream."
- Read the poems "Any Human to Another" and "A Black Man Talks of Reaping."
- Read the short story "Sweat."

Sample Daily Objectives

1. Students will learn about the concept of a dream as it related to Martin Luther King, Jr. and as it relates to themselves. Students will discuss whether Martin Luther King, Jr.'s dream has come true for African Americans in today's society and whether it has come true for them individually.
2. Students will analyze how the painting Big Meeting reflects the ideas presented in "Any Human to Another."
3. Students will learn the similarities and differences of the cultural artifact of sowing and reaping. Students will compare the view of

reaping from "A Black Man Talks of Reaping" to the ways all people of all races and creeds sow and reap.

4. Students will learn about the concept of choice. Students will analyze Delia's choice of asking white people rather than black people to help her. Discuss what choice reveals about power and race relations in Delia's community and in students' personal communities.

Sources

Teacher to choose videotape of Martin Luther King, Jr.

Bontemps, A. (1991). A black man talks to reading. In *The American experience*. Englewood Cliffs, NJ: Prentice-Hall.

Cullen, C. (1991). Any human to another. In *The American experience*. Englewood Cliffs, NJ: Prentice-Hall.

Hurston, N.Z. (1991). Sweat. In *American mosaic: Multicultural readings in context*. Boston: Houghton Mifflin.

Additional Optional Sources

Fauset, J.R. (1991). There is confusion. In *American mosaic: Multicultural readings in context*. Boston: Houghton Mifflin.

Hughes, L. (1991). The negro speaks of rivers. In *The American experience*. Englewood Cliffs, NJ: Prentice-Hall.

Locke, A. (1991). The new negro. In *American mosaic: Multicultural readings in context*. Boston: Houghton Mifflin.

Weekly Objectives, Week 5

Students will compare their own attitudes to those found in European American literature. In addition, students will become aware of stereotypical judgments and their harmful effects.

Suggested Literature Titles and Activities

Reading the short story "The Life You Save May Be Your Own." Reading the poem "Mirror."

Sample Daily Objectives

1. Students will learn about the concept of handicap as it relates to their own and others' lives. Students will discuss the ways in which Shiflet's handicap affected his behavior and the ways in which it affected other people's behavior toward him.

2. Students will compare the way Mr. Shiflet affected the Crator women tragically to ways in which someone affected their own lives either tragically or beneficially.
3. Students will analyze how the dialect in "The Life You Save May Be Your Own" may cause a reader to stereotype people speaking a different language as inferior.
4. Students will discuss the women's attitude in "Mirror" to most people's attitude toward aging.

Sources

O'Connor, F. (1991). The life you save may be your own. In *The American experience*. Englewwod Cliffs, NJ: Prentice Hall.
Plath, Sylvia. (1991). Mirror. In *The American experience*. Englewood Cliffs, NJ: Prentice-Hall.

Additional Sources

Justice, D. (1991). Poem. In *The American experience*. Englewood Cliffs, NJ: Prentice Hall.
Tyler, A. (1991). Average waves in unprotected waters. *In The American Experience*. Englewood Cliffs, NJ: Prentice-Hall.

Weekly Objectives, Week 6

Students will compare their own attitudes and values to those found in Asian drama. In addition, students will become aware of stereotypical judgments and their harmful effects as related to Asian cultures.

Suggested Drama Titles and Activities

*   Read portions of the play *Teahouse of the August Moon*.
*   Listen to the song "American dream" from *Miss Saigon*.

Sample Daily Objectives

1. Students will be exposed to stereotypes in the play. Students will compare these stereotypes to others they have come across in earlier weeks.
2. Students will define the concept of the American dream from their own perspective and as expressed in the song.
3. Students will compare the Western idea of democracy and the Eastern idea of democracy as expressed in the play.

4. Students will identify the elements in Okinawa community and the culture that Americans in the play grew to appreciate and tolerate, despite obvious differences.

Sources

Avian, B. (lyrcist). (1988). The American dream. *Miss Saigon*. New York: Geffen Records.
Patrick, J. (1963). *Teahouse of the August moon: A play*. New York: Crown.

Weekly Objectives, Week 7

Students will compare their cultural values to Hispanic cultural values. In addition, students will become aware of stereotypical judgments about the Hispanic culture.

Suggested Drama Titles and Activities

*   Read portions of the play *West Side Story* and watch portions of it on videotape.
*   Perform selected cross-cultural mini-drama from *Enucuentros Culturales*.

Sampel Daily Objectives

1. Students will compare the idea of the American dream found in last week's song to the idea of America found in the song "America" in *West Side Story*. Discuss similarities and differences.
2. Students will learn about the gangs in *West Side Story*. They will compare the gangs' similarities and differences to students' knowledge of gangs today.
3. Students will discuss the idea of gangs as related to racial prejudice. Students will also discuss the role of females in gangs, especially as related to *West Side Story*.
4. Through *West Side Story*, students will identify what machismo is within the Hispanic culture. They will compare the similarities and differences with machismo in European American culture.

Sources

Laurents, A., Bernstein, L., Sondheim, S., & Robbins, J. (1982). *West side story*. In *Introduction to theatre and drama*. Skokie, IL: National Textbook.
Snyder, B. (1977). *Encuentros culturales*. Skokie, IL: National Textbook.

Weekly Objectives, Week 8

Students will compare their attitudes and values to those found in African American drama. In addition, students will become aware of stereotypical judgments about African Americans. Students will familiarize themselves with the "American dream."

Lesson Plan Outline Week 8, Day 1

Objective. Students will identify their own dreams, hopes, and aspirations as compared with those of the characters in the play *A Raisin in the Sun* (which will be read before class). Similarities and differences will be noted.

Procedure. Students will read portions of the play aloud.

Materials. The play *A Raisin in the Sun.*

Class Assignment. After identifying the two lists of dreams (their own and the characters' in the play), students will mark similarities in the two lists and compare the Younger family's dream to the concept of the American dream discussed previously.

Evaluation.

• Participation in discussion
• Completion of written assignment

Sample Daily Objectives for Remainder of Week 8

1. Students will identify and list their values. They will compare and contrast those values to adults in their own families (journal can be used).
2. Students will identify conflicts of old and new in this story's family structure. They will identify similarities and differences and compare them to conflicts in their own family.
3. Students will explain how Water's definition of dignity changes from the beginning to the end of the play. They will discuss the similarities and differences of Water's definition of dignity compared to their own sense of dignity. In a journal entry, students will talk about their own sense of dignity.
4. Students will list examples of prejudice that the Younger family experiences. Students will compare the similarities and differences with their own lives (their perception of their own, their family's, and their community's prejudices).

Source

Hansberry, L. (1982). *A raisin in the sun*. In *Introduction to theatre and drama*. Skokie, IL: National Textbook.

Weekly Objectives, Week 9

Students will compare their own attitudes and values to those found in European American drama. In addition, students will become aware of stereotypical judgments about European Americans.

Suggested Drama Title and Activities

Read the book and watch portions of the movie *Ordinary People*.

Sample Daily Objectives

1. Students will identify the family dynamics of the Jarrett family. Students will compare and contrast similarities and differences with those of their own families.
2. Students will examine Conrad's struggle between what he feels he should be and what he actually sees himself as. In a journal entry, students will write about personal similar and different struggles of what they feel they should be versus what they perceive themselves to be.
3. Students will discuss Conrad's reaction to his brother's death and his attempted suicide. In cooperative learning groups, students will discuss why suicide has been an option of escape for people in general.
4. Students will define the Jarrett family's version of the American dream and how it was shattered. They will discuss the similarities and differences between the Jarrett family's, their own, and their family's version of the American dream. They will complete this exercise in their journals.

Source

Guest, J. (1981). Ordinary people. *Literary Cavalcade, 33*(6).

Weekly Objectives, Week 10

Based on previous discoveries concerning cultural attitudes and values, students will interpret Asian art and music.

Suggested Art/Music Titles and Activities

- Listen to the song "Living in America" by the group Hiroshima.
- "View The Great Wave of Kanagwi."
- "Critique Fugin Tomari Kyaku No Zu."
- Interpret "In Sinking Pleasure Boat."

Sample Daily Objectives

1. Students will compare and contrast similarities and differences between Asian art and music and popular art and music.
2. Students will be able to distinguish between gender roles in art and music within the Asian culture. In journals students will write on gender differences in art as they see them. This becomes a week-long assignment with library work and a possible museum trip.
3. Students will respond to Asian values through a discussion of Sinici Suzuki and his philosophies (this will take at least two classes).

Sources

Hokusai, K. (1989). *The great wave: A history of Far Eastern art*. New York: Harry N. Abrams.

Kuramoto, D., & Cortez, D. (1989). "Living in America" East. New York: CBS Records.

Teraokas, M. (1980). In sinking pleasure boat. *Portfolio Magazine, 11*.

Utamaro, K. (1978). Fugin Tomari Kyaku No Zu. *The history and process of printmaking*. New York: Holt, Rinehart & Winston.

Weekly Objectives, Week 11

Based on previous discoveries concerning cultural attitudes and values, students will interpret Hispanic art and music.

Suggested Art/Musical Works and Activities

- Critique *Si Se Puede* and *Somos Azatlan*.
- Interpret *Rope* and *People*
- Critique *Saint Francis Road Mural*.
- Listen to and then discuss *Sinfonia India*.
- Listen to and then discuss Hispanic rap and folk tunes

Sample Daily Objectives

1. Students will discover their own stereotypical judgments and prejudices through Hispanic art and folk music.
2. Students will respond through dialogue to the emotions evoked in *Rope and People* and *Sinfonia India.*
3. Students will interpret the values and attitudes found within Hispanic rap and mural paintings. In a journal entry, students will respond to the similarities and differences between Hispanic rap and rap found in their own culture.

Sources

Chavez, C. (1950). *Sinfonia India.* New York: Schimer.

Martinez E. (1991). Si Se Puede. Aquayo, Emilio. "Somos Aztlan." *Chicano Art Resistance and Affirmation,* 1965-1985. Los Angeles: UCLA Wright Art Gallery.

Miro, J. (1971). Rope and people. *Galeria Hispanica.* New York: McGraw-Hill.

Weekly Objectives, Week 12

Based on previous discoveries concerning cultural attitudes and values, students will respond to and interpret African-American art and music, comparing it to their own culture's art and music (similarities and differences).

Suggested Art/Musical Works and Activities

- Critique "Figures Drumming."
- Interpret "Christmas" and "The Dress She Wore Was Blue."
- Listen and respond to the spiritual "Didn't My Lord Deliver Daniel?"
- Listen and interpret "Jump for Joy" by Duke Ellington.

Sample Daily Objectives

1. In a journal entry, students will interpret the emotions found in the spiritual "Didn't My Lorder Deliver Daniel?"
2. In a journal entry, students will respond to their own personal experiences in relation to the aforementioned spiritual.
3. Students will respond to and interpret the Harlem renaissance through viewing "The Dress She Wore Was Blue" and "Jump for Joy."

4. Students will interpret the values and attitudes found within African-American rap and graffiti and discuss the similarities and differences to their own culture's music styles.

Sources

Hayden, P. (1987). Christmas. *Harlem renaissance art of black America.* New York: Harry N. Abrams.
Hayden, P. (1987). The dress she wore was blue. *Harlem renaissance art of black America.* New York: Harry N. Abrams.
Muntu, M. (1991). Figures drumming. *African explorers, twentieth century African art.* New York: The Center for African Art.

Weekly Objectives, Week 13

Based on previous discoveries concerning cultural attitudes and values, students will respond to and interpret European American art and music.

Suggested Art/Musical Works and Activities

- Write a story based on "Billy the Kid."
- Draw a picture based on "Putnam's Camp," Redding, Connecticut.
- Create a rap song based on real-life experiences.
- Critique "In without Knocking."
- Respond to "Untitled (Women with Softdrink)."

Sample Daily Objectives

1. Students will critique "In without Knocking" in relation to the stereotypes of the European American culture.
2. Students will discuss similar and different responses (their feelings) to experiences in "Putnam's Camp," Redding Connecticut.
3. Students will create their own rap utilizing their personal similar and different experiences. (This can be a group activity.)

Sources

Copland, A. (1958). *Billy the Kid–ballet suite.* New York: RCA Records.
Ives, C. (1958). Putnam's camp. *Three places in New England.* New York: Mercury Records.
Ruossel, (1965). In without knocking. *Artists of the Old West.* New York: Doubleday.

Unknown. (1989). *Unititled (Women with softdrink)*. Spiritual America, IVAM-Colleccio Centre del Carne.

Lesson Plan Outline Week 13, Day 1

Daily Objective.   After listening to Aaron Copland's "Billy the Kid," students will interpret the music by writing and discussing their own story or descriptive narrative in response to the music.

Procedure.

- Students will listen to an excerpt from "Billy the Kid" and will write what they feel is happening in the music.
- Students will share their responses with the rest of the class and will compare and contrast them.
- Students will write how or if the stories reflect their own reality.
- The teacher will discuss the name of the music and the story behind it.

Materials   *Billy the Kid*-Ballet Suite, Aaron Copland

Assignments.   Students will write a journal entry describing what they discovered about themselves through their interpretation of the music.

Evaluation.

- Completion of the story or narrative
- Participation in class discussion
- Completion of journal entry

Lesson Plan Outline Week 13, Day 2

Daily Objective.   By critiquing In without Knocking, students will respond to and interpret the art in relation to attitudes, values, and stereotypes of the European American culture.

Procedure.

- Review of critique and critique procedures
- Introduction to the art work "In without Knocking"
- Students will write individual responses concerning attitudes, values, and stereotypes of the culture.
- Class discussion focused on the following:

- Describe the feelings and emotions in the art work.
- What are some of the thoughts and attitudes portrayed in the art work concerning the European American culture?
- Are there any stereotypical judgments and prejudices attached to this culture? Are they visible in the art work?
- What are the reasons for the stereotypes and prejudices?
- How do you think the people of this culture feel when categorized in such a way?
- How do you feel about your prejudices? Does everyone feel this way?
- What are the similarities and differences in the way we feel about this art work?
- What changes can occur, and how, in society today, can we foster less prejudice and stereotypes.

Students should respond to some of these questions in a journal entry.

Assignment.   Students will respond to the class discussion and will relate similarities and differences within their life experiences in their own ways (words, drawings, paintings, etc.).

Evaluation.

- Participation in class discussion
- Completion of the artistic sketch

Other Sources

Anderson, W. (1991). *Teaching music with a multicultural approach.* Reston, VA: MENC: The National Association for Music Education.

Floyd, S.A., (Ed.). (1990). *Black music in the Harlem renaissance: A collection of essays.* Westport, CT: Greenwood.

Hermann, E., & Sinichi, S. (1981). *The man and his philosophy.* Athens, OH: Accura Music.

Koskoff, E. (Ed.). (1987). *Women and music in cross cultural perspective.* Westport, CT: Greenwood.

Additional Art Sources

Berliner, N. (1995). Chinese papercuts. *American Craft, 45*(2), 16-21.

The Bronx Museum of the Arts. (1988). *The Latin American spirit: Art and artists in the United States, 1920-1970.* New York: Harry N. Abrams.

Glueckert, A. (1989). Sumi-e painting. *Schools Arts,* 27-29.

Lee, S. (1983). Realism in Japanese art: Things of this world and no other. *Portfolio Magazine, 5*(2), 62-67.

Mendelowitz, D.M. (1970). *A history of American art.* New York: Holt, Rinehart & Winston.

Schuman, J.M. (1981). *Art from many hands: Multicultural art projects for home and school.* Englewood Cliffs, NJ: Prentice Hall.

Sugimura, Y. (1966). *Chinese sculpture bronzes, and jades in Japanese collections.* Honolulu: East-West Center Press.

Week 14, Unit Conclusion

On completion of this unit, students will synthesize their heightened awareness of self, stereotypes, prejudices, and the various voices within the four cultures into a group presentation. The focus of the presentation will be similarities within differences and multiculturalism. Sample activities may include poetry readings, skits, vocal selections, slide shows, and dance performances. The presentation will be performed first in the school and then possibly within the district, if arranged. If possible, performances in other school districts and for community groups will follow.

CONCLUSION

On one level, this curriculum development attempt has been a humbling experience. In a curriculum document of any sort, no mention is made of the conscious attempt of teachers to challenge race, class, and gender disparities and formulate a curriculum of inclusion that attempts to challenge forms of oppression, alienation and subordination. On another level, curriculum development of this variety can provide guidelines, hints, possibilities and hopes on what it might take to inject curriculum with a politics of inclusion. Thus, what is represented in this chapter is merely both an example and the tip of the iceberg in helping guide teachers (and ourselves) in helping to make the classroom a space of inclusion. I am convinced that content areas such as social studies, arts, music, humanities, history, English, math and so on can be the beneficiaries of a curriculum that uses inclusion and its various aligning concepts as a theoretical and parochial framework for the teaching–learning process.

II

EDUCATIONAL REFORM

6

Tensions Related to Inclusion within the 1990s Reform Movement in Mathematics and Science

Thomas E. McDuffie

Saint Joseph's University

The reform movement in mathematics (M) and science (S) education (MS reform) is not just important, but is critical to this treatise on inclusion! Its centrality begins to flow from the fact that mathematics is required of almost all K–12 student every year. Of greater consequence, MS reform represents a turbid and turbulent confluence of theory and practice where the social concerns of critical pedagogy—social equality, gender equity, and multiculturalism—are in tension with the mainstream concerns—academic tradition, intellectual integrity, and discipline-based standards. Overall, the restructuring of MS education, and the accompanying technology (T) issues, provides the broadest, best conceived, and best documented example of a national movement that embraced inclusive concepts and approaches, and attempted to apply them to clearly defined, core academic disciplines.

Viewing reform through the lens of inclusion reveals a series of "points of tension" traceable to age-old positions that pit the academic goals of education against its social goals. Inclusion brings the social and academic goals of reform into sharp contrast around age-old educational questions. Is the central purpose of schools to communicate or transform society? Is the central function of the schools social or academic? Are the issues of excellence and equal opportunity paradoxical or contradictory? The central role of education was described, debated, and defined both implicitly and explicitly. The process and products of reform are arguably the engineering of ideas and ideals within the constraints of probability and practicality. Various interpretations of curriculum ideas, instructional priorities, evaluative techniques, and priorities had to be addressed and resolved. During the creation of a reforms vision, the perceived social and intellectual needs of the nation competed, and the balance between quality and equity had to be calibrated. A number of paradoxes loomed near the surface of the movement that could only be negotiated politically. For example, the concepts of equality versus excellence, and multiculturalism versus the culture of mathematics and science had proponents tugging in opposite directions. Not to be forgotten is the tension between depth and breadth of content that led the Third International Mathematics and Science Study (TIMSS) to decry America's curricula as "A mile wide and an inch deep"!

Two volumes present the major goals of the MS reform movement. The very titles of the "social beacons"—*Everybody Counts* and *Science for All Americans*—proclaim a commitment to multiculturalism, egalitarianism, and democracy rare, perhaps new, to any major redirection of curriculum and instruction in U.S. history. The cover photograph of *Everybody Counts* depicts America's future scientists and mathematicians as more minority than majority, more female than male, and more dark skinned than light. The text embodies the key theme of reform and proposed a set of academic standards that

> constitute a common core of learning in science, mathematics, and technology for all of young people, regardless of this social circumstances and career aspirations. In particular, the recommendations pertain to those who in the past have been largely bypassed in science and mathematics education: ethnic and language minorities and girls. (AAAS, 1990, xviii)

Initially, this stance seemed more politically motivated than philosophically justified. Linkages between the movement's inclusive concepts and social theory or philosophical notions of social justice were indirect. However, as the millennium dawns a re-examination of this issue has elevated the theoretical role of social principles.

Economic participation of all youngsters through education is a powerful, clearly stated end. At the same time, the content integrity of the academic disciplines and the role of intellectual pursuit in the development of thought had been preserved. That said, reform's strategy acknowledges the need for pragmatism and political savvy. The broad-based movement was forged through a combination of power and negotiated process that joined federal and state agencies with professional organizations. Its fuel was federal financial support often funneled through state departments of education. Its keystone was and remains the desire to prepare all children to participate successfully in the emerging economy. Empowering children mathematically, scientifically, and technologically will enable them to enjoy our nation's economic success during their lives.

Of principal concern to this chapter is an analysis of tensions evident in several major aspects of the movement. Two theses underlie the argument:

1. At the core of reform and throughout most of its manifestations, the movement is more evolutionary than revolutionary; more egalitarian than elitist and more focused on outcomes than inputs.
2. Reform is championed as a vehicle "for all Americans," but the implementation strategy and the nature of the disciplines suggests that it is more egalitarian than inclusive.

The transformation of these theses into a well-clad argument is the aim of this presentation. It begins with an analysis of the changes occurring within MS education followed by a detailed look at the antecedents of reform and the role of assessment within it that includes contrasts between present movement and prior efforts. Then it examines inclusive factors implicit in "all children" such as gender, multiculturalism, and empowerment and their relation to curriculum, instruction, and learning. It concludes with an examination of approaches currently being used to modify and improve America's classroom achievement.

BACKGROUND TO REFORM

A macroscopic examination of the movement reveals that the current MS reformation was constructed on several broadly conceived tenets. First, the movement projects a relatively long, perhaps on-going image, unlike the concrete timeline that existed during the curricula projects of the 1960s. The intended audience for change, for example, extends well beyond the present population toward youngsters, which demographics tells us will fill America's classrooms for future decades, perhaps as long as the next half century. Second, achieving the desired goals necessitates very basic systemic, classroom, and instructional changes. Strategically assessment will drive curriculum and instruction. Third, instructional approaches proposed by reform actually reflect a century or more of teaching/learning and includes many of John Dewey's axioms. Fourth, the accelerated rate change occurring in science, mathematics, and technological limits content selection to central, enduring concepts as well as facility with the processes of inquiry. Finally, and of great importance to national acceptance, the present movement exhibits significant political insight, costs taxpayers little, and provides an avenue for maintaining local control.

Examination of the current MS reform effort, any major educational endeavor actually, should include questions whose answers ultimately provide guidance for future efforts designed to improve education. A backdrop to the present analysis is the harmony between its proclaimed goals, the reality of the classroom and historic precedents. Where does the initiative come from? How is it related to and different from prior reformations in mathematics and science? Are goals realistic and attainable? What does "all children" mean? Will the most or least able students suffer academically? Will the integrity of the disciplines in terms of rigor and achievement remain in tact? Will the necessary resources for change be made available? Will a national initiative co-opt states rights? As the German idiom suggests "God is in the details!"

Coupling a firsthand view of the reform movement in MST with a review of the literature leads to the identification of 10 strands that shape most aspects of the movement. These factors provide a skeletal guide that both summarizes the background to reform and provide a springboard to its varied manifestations. Together they paint a picture of a movement that was informed by past events and efforts as well as one keenly aware of the societal conditions at the end of the 20th century.

1. Linkage to *A Nation at Risk*, the clarion call to improve the education of young Americans, and *Goals 2000*, the financial and political catalyst enabling national change.
2. Conviction that all children can learn science and mathematics bolstered by an awareness of demographic realities of a changing population.
3. Financial support and leadership from overlapping governmental agencies, political factions, and economic forces, as well as cross-pollination in committee membership.
4. Recognition of society's increased needs and demands for well-prepared individuals who are ready and able to enter the workforce and contribute to their communities.
5. Realization that elitist, "teacher-proof" curricula developed by subject area specialists during the post Sputnik era proved wanting.
6. Acceptance of standards based education as the most effective and least costly approach to improving education.

7. Agreement on "literacy"—mathematical or scientific—as the aspiration for all change.
8. Use of authentic assessment to stimulate curriculum and instructional change.
9. Acceptance of an integrated, constructivist learning paradigm.
10. Promotion of active learning to modify and improve classroom instruction, and the incorporation of instruction that enhances learning.

HISTORIC CONTEXT OF REFORM

Our very success as humans is linked to the transmission of shared values, mores, attitudes, and skills from one generation to the next that long predated formal schools. Since Colonial times, America's schools were intended to complement, reinforce, and extend the efforts of family, religion, and other social institutions. Complex political, social realities coupled with philosophical and religious beliefs form a matrix within which schools exist, evolve, and perform their central functions. Family, culture, religion, peers, books, media, and life experiences in general each help shape students' values toward knowledge, learning, and schools. As the influence of religion and community wane, schools' social responsibility has broadened to subsume areas formerly the domain of family, community, and religion.

> Historically, schools in the United States were designed with a dual mission: to teach all students basic skills required for a lifetime of work in an industrial and agricultural economy and to educate a small elite who would go to college en route to professional careers. As the needs of society have changed—as a function of students preparing to work in factories or on farms has declined—the balance of these two goals has shifted. (AAAS, 1990, p. 11)

Although today's social reality, as well as the academic vitality of America's schools, test the very paradigm on which public education rests. Education's central role, from the viewpoint of the reform movement, is conservative. That is, its fundamental goal is to communicate, not change society. Increasingly participatory democracy will depend on the skills, processes and knowledge gained in the classroom. Thus, Goodman (1995) described the present reform as third wave restructuring to meet the needs of the information technology age rather than a profound, transformation of education. Societal evolution occurs gradually through individual empowerment not from external, transformative forces.

Full participation in the current technological revolution and success over a lifetime demand higher levels of skills, thinking ability and communication than in previous historic eras. "The world of work in the twenty-first century will be less manual but more mental; less mechanical but more electronic; less routine but more verbal; and less static but more varied" (National Research Council, 1989, p. 11). No longer are the skills that sufficed on barn or factory floors adequate. Economic freedom and the personal dignity it enhances demand a solid foundation of enduring intellectual and social skills including the ability to learn throughout a lifetime. Functional illiteracy, when it persists, will be a millstone causing personal isolation and financial disenfranchisement for the individual; further polarization for the society; and competitive disadvantages in the international market place.

The interplay between mathematics, science, technology, and society is inescapable in the current MS reform movement. The economic imperative woven through the 1980s anthem of reform, *A Nation at Risk* (1983), and the beacons of the present MS reform, *Everybody Counts* (NCR, 1989), and *Science for All Americans* (AAAS, 1990), highlights the relationship between individuals, schools, and society. A prime social concern was to protect America's position within the world economy and provide opportunity for individuals to enjoy the fruits of their accomplishment. Within this framework, *Science for All Americans* outlines an educational vehicle to carry all children into the mainstream.

In setting the educational course, reform leaders elevated scientific and mathematical literacy beyond all other goals. The need for a solid foundation of knowledge in an increasingly technical world was proclaimed using charged language.

> *Science for All Americans* is based on the belief that the science-literate person is one who is aware that science, mathematics, and technology are interdependent human enterprises with strengths and limitations; understands key concepts and principles of science; is familiar with the natural world and recognizes both its diversity and unity; and uses scientific knowledge and scientific ways of thinking for individual and social purposes. (AAAS, 1990, p. xvii)

In the broad view, multiple dimensions of literacy can be identified. The National Research Council (NRC) chose four basic strands: "Functional literacy, in all of its manifestations—verbal, mathematical, scientific, and cultural—provides a common fabric of communication indispensable for modern civilized society" (NRC, 1989, p. 8). In reform documents, the commonality between science and mathematical literacy was discussed in detail; that between culture and these dimensions was not laid bare.

Academically, today's schools labor under the legacy of the structure designed for the industrial age misapplied to educate children for the information age. One academic manifestation of the assembly line mentality is the structural compartmentalization of knowledge into rigid subject areas. A prime example is the extreme stance of the 1960s when mathematics and science were presented as pure, theoretical, self-contained entities detached from each other as well as the real world. In an attempt to develop a generation of theoretical scientists, curricula of the era, including most sponsored by the National Science Foundation, expunged the very examples of technology from physics and chemistry that bonded the disciplines to their industrial and historic origins. Theory often filled the void, leaving capable students without the concrete examples necessary to understand concepts, and less able with no meaningful reference points at all.

In declaring literacy the ultimate goal, today's reformers emphasized the mutually supportive aspects of the subject areas both in terms of curriculum and content. In fact, the interweaving of science and mathematics education is so total politically, practically, and strategically that the movement is usually viewed as one. The individual disciplines may be envisioned as the legs of a ladder and the interrelationships as rungs that make conceptual understanding richer. In a parallel sense, during the last quarter of the 19th century, both mathematics and science became increasingly dependent on technology for their new discoveries, whereas the reverse was the case earlier.

> It is the union of science, mathematics, and technology that forms the scientific endeavor and that makes it so successful. Although each of these human enterprises has a character and history of its own, each is dependent on and reinforces the other. (AAAS, 1990, p. 1)

Although school practices have emphasized the distinctness of the science and mathematics in the past to suggest that the integration of mathematics and science is a new curriculum concept would be misleading. It is not! Physics teachers have long included instruction in mathematics when was needed just as biology teachers presented chemical principles. In a more formal but limited sense, two programs developed in the 1960s integrated the disciplines—School Mathematics Study Group (SMSG) and The Minnesota School Mathematics and Science Center (MINNEMAST). It is the degree of the overlap between mathematics and science coupled with the embracing of technology that is novel to today's rebirth. Using the words of program directors, "Mathematics is especially critical because mathematics is the language of science and technology" (NRC, 1989, p. 8).

A STRATEGY FOR NATIONAL CHANGE

The strategy for change was conceived on a national level, but the specific manifestations of the process and plans for achieving goals are a state and local function. In 1989, the nation's governors adopted the National Education Goals that became the basis for the Clinton Administration's *Goals 2000: Educate America Act.* After input from stakeholders—taxpayers to teachers, and parents to politicians—a set of standards was developed for the nation's K–12 schools. National Council of Teachers of Mathematics (NCTM) Standards became the currency for mathematics while the National Science Education Standards (NSES) served to guide changes in the sciences and technology. Standards described the knowledge, skills, and understanding needed so that "By the year 2000, U.S. students will be first in the world in mathematics and science achievement." Generally, these markers provide gateposts for student achievement at the transition stages (i.e., the completion of the primary grades, middle school, and high school). National standards outline what all students should know and be able to do to live and work in the 21st century; thus, provide state and local educators with targets they could adapt or adopt.

Implementation of academic standards, although not unprecedented (Hiebert, 1999), is a milestone in America's educational history. In the salons of politics where setting goals translates simultaneously into their attainment and teacher accountability, standards have attained a Bunyanesque stature. In local school districts, standards provide a yardstick for determining worthiness of content to be included in courses of study, appropriateness of instructional approaches, allocation on instructional time, and flow of resources.

In a departure from earlier approaches, curriculum was defined to include three interrelated components: standards, assessment, and instruction. Fiscally, conservatism ruled! Few additional federal or state dollars were needed to implement the plan as few additional funds went to local districts. State departments of education worked with discipline-based organizations to recast, publicize, and promote standards. Commonly, statewide testing programs were established on a state's standards to determine achievement on both a state and local level. Evaluation was designed to drive both the enacted curriculum and instruction. Scores on state-level tests were the major factors in determining local districts, schools, and even individual teacher's accomplishments. Results were framed as a statement of school or district quality. Strategically, pragmatism reigned! "If it is on the test, it will be taught." When scores are low, instruction must be focused and time increased.

In establishing national mathematics standards, the NCTM had a comparatively easy task because mathematics educators have more uniform disciplinary roots. Mathematics standards, therefore, resulted primarily from the codification of ideas from a single group. Science educators whose ranks include students of the physical, biological, and earth sciences faced a larger task. The NRC's effort to create the NSES began with bridging the chasm between the widely different, sometimes opposing viewpoints developed by the National Science Teacher's Association and the American Association for the Advancement of Science. The ultimate goal was to ensure well-educated, scientifically sophisticated future citizenry.

The creation of standards became a point of tension between some champions of inclusion who hold that the implementation of standards is discriminatory and inherently wrong. Reformers rejected this notion, but recognized that the establishment of standards may appear exclusive because their assessment distinguishes between the performance and demonstrated knowledge of individuals. To them, academic standards are by design and intent criterion for judging expertise not innate human worth. Setting and implementing standards in MS, although both political and value-laden, is hardly immoral. It is neither related to nor parallels exclusive acts like eliminating individual participation by race, gender, or orientation (Hiebert, 1989). The latter is a violation of basic human principles — democracy, dignity, and worth; the former is an evaluative process based on professionally accepted principles for estimating skill or knowledge levels. "We can debate the merits of particular standards and criteria, and particular understandings, interpretations, and applications of them, of course. But we cannot reject standards and criteria altogether — not, at least, if we wish to uphold the value of inclusion" (Siegel, 1995, p. 11). To dismiss standards is to deny individuals the privilege of their personal accomplishments and its companion recognition.

INCLUSIVE FACTORS AND REFORM:
CHOICE, MULTICULTURALISM AND GENDER

Four central elements link reform to the guiding concept of this book: choice, inclusion of all youngsters, multiculturalism, and gender equity. Although distinct in their manifestations, each factor provides highly visible social markers that indicate the extent to which MS education is being made more available, meaningful and democratic.

Students' Decisions

No personal choice is more debilitating than a student's decision not to learn to the best of his or her ability. The widely accepted constructivist notion of learning lays bare the relationship between teaching and learning. As expressed by the NRC (1989), "no one can *teach* mathematics. Effective teachers are those who can stimulate students to *learn* mathematics" (p. 58). Implicit in the constructivist paradigm, but too rarely examined, is the responsibility for learning this requires the student. Individual choice and circumstances, whether culturally embedded, socially motivated, or personality driven, cannot be dominated by external forces alone. Given an internal locus of control, students must assume responsibility for decisions. If an individual chooses, for whatever reason, not to attend school or participate in classes, then the individual's potential to learn will diminish. If shackled by circumstances that inhibit active learning, the individual's potential to learn will not be realized. If classroom efforts are minimal, attempts to meet academic standards will fall short; and educational, social, and economic doors will close.

No factor threatens future academic success, creates a higher barrier to economic participation, or excludes more individuals from the mainstream than ill-informed or easy course choices made during the middle grades. Consequently, a national debate has begun over mandating algebra for all students because less than one third of the students who do not take algebra matriculate in college. Algebra is the "gateway" to advanced MS work. A healthy 83% of students who took both algebra and geometry enrolled in college within 2 years of their scheduled high school graduation (U.S. Department of Education, 1997). Students who avoid mathematics courses on the secondary level or who take diluted substitutes such as "advanced arithmetic" or "commercial mathematics" choose disenfranchisement. Whether self-imposed, or stemming from little or no academic guidance, the most probable result of poor choices, especially low-income, ethnic minority, at-risk students, is a form of economic, intellectual, and social exile.

All Young People

Is the establishment of standards "for all of young people, regardless of their social circumstances and career aspirations," a vaporous, political statement, or a realistic and attainable goal? Response aside, the question highlights the single greatest challenge facing inclusive education today. Given the conceptually abstract nature of advanced mathematics and science, can students who have not and possibly will never develop logical, abstract thinking function at a high level in these disciplines? Will individuals with significant ability but low interest or facility with the disciplines succeed within them? Does equal opportunity lead to equal outcomes?

Clearly, the authors of *Everybody Counts* (NRC, 1989) wrestled with these questions. They were pulled in one direction by the forces accompanying the broad, cultural/social spectrum of youngsters in the nation's public and nonpublic schools, and in the other by the cognitive demands of advanced mathematics and science. Unlike the elitist, post-Sputnik initiatives of the 1960s when the creation of scientists was the objective, an openly egalitarian position was taken that offers full participation in MS education to all youngsters. It is believed that educating the broad spectrum of today's youth will serve society at large better than an elitist education for the gifted. Recommendations, however, were "deliberately ambitious, for it would be worse to under estimate what students can learn than to expect too much" (AAAS, 1990, p. xviii). Yet, being number one in the world—elitism—while meeting the needs of all students—egalitarianism—has proven futile and remains a point of tension. Moreover, it has contributed to the demand for recasting of the mathematics standards in states like California a mere decade after their initial publication.

Early reform committees proposed the impossible—being "all things to all people." The operational definition the AAAS selected for "all children" sheds dappled light on the interpretation of and commitment to inclusion within the movement. In what must have been a harrowing, difficult to negotiate decision, "all children" became, for all practical purposes, "some children." "Given clear goals, the right resources, and good teaching throughout 13 years of school—essentially all students (operational meaning 90 percent or more) will be able to reach all the recommended learning goals (meaning at least 90 percent) by the time they graduate from high school" (AAAS, 1990, p. xviii). Such a blatantly operational stance replaces the philosophical or social principals of inclusion with realistic, and political ones of pragmatism. In effect, the definition of all children exposes the very underbelly of society that it intends to elevate through changes in curriculum and instruction. In a graduating class of 300, an entire 30-student homeroom could fail, but the program still would be considered a success. Predictably, these youngsters come from the economically challenged or minority cultures. Worse, reaching the recommended learning goals at the proficiency level as interpreted by many states is often less than challenging.

Several years into the reformation, major questions remain unresolved and issues debated only superficially. Is U.S. education's prime concern with the development of individual potential, large or small, or is it tied to the elitist notion of being the best? Are we trying to be the best or are we for "all children"? Any leaning toward one side of the issue or the other creates a maelstrom of protest. One observation seems to beg the obvious, either reform's target is out of focus and its aim is low, or the cognitive demands of MS defy universal standards.

Multiculturalism

Reformers clearly recognized the cultural matrix within which SMT evolved and mandated study of the historical origin of ideas to enhance student literacy. From a pragmatic, instructional viewpoint, sharing generalizations generated by mathematical or scientific approaches to problem solving becomes impossible without concrete examples to build on. From a scholarly perspective, the history of scientific thought contributes to our cultural heritage and provides personal points of identity such as role models for youngsters.

Although highly intertwined within the standards, historically mathematics, science, and technology evolved rather independently of each other. Mathematics is arguably the most universal of the trio and science the least. Basic mathematics grew from an amalgam of ideas representing every corner of the globe. Science, traceable to the empirical approach of Francis Bacon, developed under the most limited circumstances. With technical roots in Asia and a saving history in North Africa during Europe's Dark Ages, the philosophical roots of the scientific endeavor are European, rational, and male. The thought process is particularly Western. The empirical testing of hypothetical or logical statements through observation and controlled experimentation, loosely recognized as the "scientific method," has proven profoundly influential on today's world. Speculation about how greater diversity including more involvement of women would have shaped and improved the enterprise is fun, but fruitless (Ross, 1996).

Given the extent of European influence, it does not seem unreasonable that recommendations in the standards

> focus on the development of science, mathematics, and technology in Western culture, but not on how that development drew on ideas from earlier Egyptian, Chinese, Greek, and Arabic cultures. The sciences as accounted for in this report are largely part of a tradition of thought that happened to develop in Europe during the last five hundred years—a tradition to which people of all cultures contribute today. (AAAS, 1990, p. 145)

Through time and across continents, people have engaged in technological activities as well as mathematical and scientific endeavors. The extent to which they used each varied based on their needs, interests, economic pursuits, and leisure time. Ancient technologies such as prehistoric people's toolkits are fascinating, but tangential to the current issue. More pertinent is how major civilizations counted objects, measured quantities, explained events, invented calendars, and described the passage of time. Ancient artistic patterns, building plans, and games are a few of the ways mathematical concepts were involved in early cultures. Because each society, each group may have solved problems slightly differently many may take credit for some form of technological invention.

Cultural infusion has resulted in wholesale adoption or adaptation of the most successful concepts. Over time, ownership of basic mathematical concepts and approaches became more universal than distinctive. Our very number system, for example, originated in India and entered Europe through Arabic-speaking North Africans. Much of the mathematics America's children learn in elementary and middle school can be traced to Greece, Africa, and Asia. More than 5,000 years ago, the Egyptians were using a system of written numerals based on grouping by tens. But, like the Mayan system developed in our own hemisphere, it is beyond the mainstream of mathematics. Too many of the geometric relationships studied in high school were formalized in ancient Greece. The abacus, an honorable antecedent of today's calculator, has been used in Asian countries for centuries. The history of concepts is promoted less for scientific and mathematical reasons than to encourage multicultural perspectives. Tracing MS concepts enrich students' learning by adding a broad, humanistic view.

In a very profound sense, the nature of mathematics, science, and technology present a challenge the attainment of the inclusive principles set forth by reforms. Modern mathematics and science are neither as culturally bound nor as culturally rooted as history, literature, and art. Mathematics, from the perspective of language, is culturally neutral in comparison with other modern languages. Chanting the Arabic numerals in any language is less emotionally charged than any anthem in the same tongue. From the frame of reference of the national standards, mathematics, science, and technology embody a distinctive set of values as well as highly prized skills that enhance and shape today's society.

> Thus, to the degree that schooling concerns itself with values and attitudes—a matter of great sensitivity in the society that prizes cultural diversity and individuality and is wary of ideology—it must take scientific values and attitudes into account when preparing young people for life beyond school. Similarly, there are certain thinking skills associated with science, mathematics, and technology that young people need to develop during their school years. These are mostly, but not exclusively, mathematical and logical skills that are essential tools for both formal and informal learning and for a lifetime of participation in schools as a whole. (AAAS, 1990, p. 183)

The Gender Gap

Significant differences in the achievement scores of males and females, as well as their interest in science and mathematics, were so common until the 1970-1980s that they were considered natural. Although a host of sexist hypotheses pretended to explain the chasm, equal opportunity and exposure to the disciplines have made these explanations wither. Gender-related differences in achievement and enrollment in mathematics have vanished in

K–12. The TIMSS and the National Assessment of Educational Progress (NAEP) both found no discernable difference between the mathematics performance of boys and girls in Grades 4 and 8. Differences in science results and interest linger, such as on the fourth-grade science achievement (National Education Goals Panel, 1997), but have decreased dramatically over the last 15 years. Although nothing less than equality is acceptable, the significant chasm between test scores of males and females has vanished. Arguments about environmental constraints associated with the socialization of girls and boys, once compelling, are now less resonant. No longer are differences in career aspirations acceptable. Any hint of genetic differences in ability and subsequent accomplishment is vanishing. Of all major reform-related educational accomplishments in the last decade or so, none exceeds the shrinking of the gender gap as reflected in the achievement scores in MS.

ACHIEVING NATIONAL STANDARDS

Determining the ultimate goals of the MS reform movement—being the best in the world in MS achievement or ensuring that all children reach high standards—has proven more difficult than describing the process for attaining the standards (see Fig. 6.1). In the simplest form, three aspects of curriculum operating within a learning environment, set the stage for high achievement.

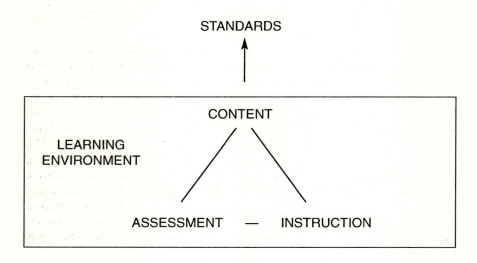

Figure 6.1. Model for Achieving Standards

Assessment, content, and instruction are interdependent aspects of curriculum that can lead to success within an appropriate environment. In this model, standards define the skills, processes, knowledge, and understandings that students should be able to demonstrate at given grade levels. They provide a perspective that lends it self to measurement. Assessing standards profoundly influences both the selection of content and the instructional approaches that promote success. In essence, assessment of standards shapes and focuses the learning environment.

ASSESSMENT ISSUES WITHIN REFORM

National and state agencies have avoided prescribing local curriculum and instructional procedures and have limited their financial support of local professional development or curricular initiatives. Change is driven by testing, not dollars. Pragmatism reigned, "If it is on the test, it will be taught!" State departments of education developed and implemented testing programs with the support of federal money then rewarded Local Educational Authorities (LEAs) based on test scores. Scores on state-level tests are the major factor in determining local districts, schools, and even individual teacher's accomplishments. Results are framed and shared in the press as indicators of school or district successes. In effect, states have used test results to leverage change as opposed to providing local districts with the resources needed to achieve the standards. When scores are generally low, the strategy can backfire as instruction tends to be focused on the three Rs and time on reading increased.

Two approaches to measurement take opposite tacks in the winds of assessment reform. Authentic approaches to assessment, and standardized tests of high technical quality are points of tension because they occupy opposite ends of the evaluation continuum as well as contrasting psychological positions. Authentic, constructivist-based assessment is best used at the district or school level where the local curriculum is addressed and individual students have multiple opportunities to demonstrate proficiency. The content and format of such instruments promotes attainment of learning outcomes by reflecting good instruction (Simon, 1995). True to its formative nature, classrooms become laboratories for action research in which teachers can modify content, learning experiences, and the format of instruction to fit a test's profile. The high level of synergy between this mode of assessment and the reform movement's goals and constructivist underpinnings is obvious.

Group testing at the national, state, or district level has traditionally been summative. Its primary goal is to measure performance for accountability purposes in one form and another. Within this framework, technical measurement issues such as validity, reliability, and bias become paramount. When denial of a high school diploma or admission to a prestigious and rewarding career track is based on the score of a single assessment strategy, for example, evaluative instruments must meet very stringent technical quality criteria. Even when the highest psychometric characteristics have been attained, debate can rage over predictable outcomes in achievement related to economic, cultural, or racial group.

Confusion erupts when policymakers use the same instrument for both purposes, thereby creating a conflict between the formative evaluation that can guide instruction and technical quality demanded of an external summative evaluation. The former assesses individual performance against local or state-level standards; the latter contrasts performance against that of a norm group. In any environment where outcomes are based on standardized tests, language and cultural differences as well as economic status are highly correlated with results.

CONTENT AND TEXTBOOKS

Initial emphasis on standards and assessment has migrated toward curricular issues. The TIMSS group led a rising chorus of dissidents who reject current textbooks and may soon call for massive curriculum projects.

> The present curricula in science and mathematics are over stuff and undernourished. Over the decades, they have grown with little restraint; thereby overwhelming teachers and students and making it difficult for them to keep track of what science, mathematics, and technology is truly essential. Some topics are taught over and over again in needless detail; some that are of equal or greater importance to science literacy — often from the physical and social sciences and from technology — are absent from the curriculum or are reserved for only a few students. (AAAS, 1989, pp. xv-xvi)

Very different manifestations of this problem are found in M and S textbook programs — the informal, national curricula. Until the late 1980s mathematics curriculum and instruction exhibited more stagnation then dynamism. The "new math" of the 1960s was misunderstood and cursed by many whose encounters seemed little more than theoretical mysteries. To an astonishing degree, the mathematics curriculum of the early 1980s reflected the Committee of Ten's recommendations made at the end of the 19th century. Their plan, a conceptual hierarchy with calculus at the pinnacle, constrained any introduction of mathematics topics found in today's world of science, technology, commerce, and daily living. Calculus no longer provides a comfortable, ultimate terminus for all early mathematics; standard algorithms no longer provide a reliable guide to mathematical applications; and facility with arithmetic no longer represents mathematical literacy.

> As mathematics is more than calculation, so education in mathematics must be more than mastery of arithmetic. Geometry, chance, and change are as important as basic operations in achieving mathematical power. Even more important is a comprehensive, flexible view that embodies the intrinsic unity of mathematics: estimation supplements calculation, heuristics aid algorithms, and experience balances innovation. To prepare students to use mathematics in the twenty-first century, today's curriculum must invoke the full spectrum of the mathematical sciences. (AAAS, 1989, p. 43)

Science curricula, by contrast, contain too many distinct ideas. Loss of focus permitted the addition of a wide range of popular, but tangential ideas that became new chapters in the "revised" editions. The typical U.S. science text covers between 53 and 67 topics, depending on the grade level, whereas in Germany texts concentrate on nine topics and Japan's texts stress 8 to 17 topics. This accretion led the TIMSS group to announce publicly that science textbooks and prevalent methods of instruction

> actually impede rather than promote science literacy by emphasizing the learning of answers more than the exploration of questions; by testing bits and pieces of information instead of exploring understandings; by instructing at a memory level at the expense of enhancing critical thought; by concentrating on reading in lieu of doing. (Schmidt, McKnight, & Raizen, 1999, p. 3)

A similar contrast in depth was evident: The five most emphasized topics in U.S. fourth-grade science textbooks account for 25% of the average textbook compared to the international average of 70% to 75% (Science and Engineering Indicators, pp. 1-19). The description "A mile wide and an inch deep" has more than a poetic ring.

PEDAGOGY, TEACHERS, AND THE CONDITIONS OF LEARNING

To a surprising degree, the pedagogical soul of the reform movement is anchored in the 19th not the 20th century. "Effective Learning and Teaching," the principal statement on pedagogy in *Science for All Americans* (AAAS, 1990), reads like a progressive educator's primer on desirable instructional strategies. Prominent, guiding ideas that Dewey might embrace include problem-based learning solved by students working cooperatively, real-world relevance, relating content to interest and experience, interdisciplinary teaching, and recognition that people construct meaning and understandings. Darling-Hammond's (1993) generic comments about contemporary reform are particularly applicable to mathematics and science education: "With the addition of a few computers, John Dewey's 1900 vision of the 20th-century ideal is virtually identical to the current scenarios for 21st-century schools" (p. 755). Dewey lost his initial battle for transforming the schools, but the orientation of reformers on most of the points of tension indicate that his impact has been profound. Certainly, the democratic principles he espoused have been embraced and the instructional philosophy he proposed has been adapted as anchors of reform.

Historically, the focus of instruction in U.S. education was on teachers' actions, strategies, and use of resources. Today's instructional paradigm centers on student learning. Teachers are no longer primarily transmitters of knowledge; rather, they facilitate the learning process. They (a) incorporate classroom activities that encourage students to express how they approach problems both orally and in writing; (b) engage students in the human aspects of mathematics and science that necessitate cooperative, team approaches to solve problems; and (c) promote the construction of meaning (NRC, 1990). To reach the goal of enhancing learning for all students, effective teaching must reflect the nature of the disciplines as well as current findings about how students learn mathematics and science. Providing challenging opportunities for all students demands implementation of a range of teaching strategies to accommodate diversity and to encourage construction of individual understanding of concepts. Expertise in the discipline is merely a first step for teachers who must increasingly relate diverse learner characteristics and needs with curriculum and instructional planning.

The learning environment embraced by reformers may appear Utopian to some, but for others, including a disproportionate number of today's urban teachers and children, it is pure fantasy. Classroom observations and teacher comments confirm that efforts to control behavior often exceed efforts to instruct. Instructional strategies are chosen with a careful eye on behavioral management. Creativity, problem solving, and understanding are abandoned to avoid disruptions. Thus, exercises incorporated into instruction emphasize drill and emulation rather than practice strategies and extend meaning. In effect, teachers provide a time sponge that channels potentially disruptive energy regardless of its source—boredom, lack of interest, or frustration—toward an intellectually noncorruptive task. Past emphasis on procedural knowledge and repetition reflected well on older standardized tests that limited items to the knowledge level. Today, "Skills are to mathematics what scales are to music or spelling is to writing. The objective of learning is to write, to play music, or to solve problems—not just to master skills" (NRC, 1989, p. 57). To thrive in the technology-laden world of the next century knowledge of skills is merely a starting point and overemphasis of them can shackle youngsters to the past.

Approaches to infuse multiculturalism into the classroom, a significant effort within the reform movement, exemplify the methods used to make MS more appealing and culturally relevant to underserved populations. Related articles have been published in many issues of the major journals sponsored by the NCTM and the National Science Teacher's Association. *Focus,* the official voice of Eisenhower National Clearinghouse, has championed multiculturalism and gender concerns. In a distilled sense, major classroom recommendations revolve around knowledge of student backgrounds, culture, and interests; the use of culturally related examples and models to promote learning; and the implementation of active learning strategies. None of these changes either the standards-related content emphasis or level of abstractness; each, however, forges links between learners and content. Several examples of widely applicable classroom suggestions merit consideration.

While specifically addressing instructional practices to bolster learning among Asian American children, Feng (1994) shared long-recognized, but ever sound advice. Teachers should familiarize themselves with the religious and cultural traditions of their students and base academic expectations on individual ability rather than on stereotypes. Asian descent, she stressed, is no better predictor of mathematical prowess than another heritage forecasts mathematical doom. She further suggested that the complexity of a multicultural classroom is compounded by the fact that the disciplines of science have their own culture and language.

Taking a step beyond cultural sensitivity, Gallard (1992) noted that learning is facilitated by providing students with opportunities to make sense of science phenomena through varied, multisensory experiences. This very notion, doing math and science, is almost a mantra of reformers. Although common to science instruction, an active approach to mathematics education that includes the use of manipulatives, real-world problems, calculators, and computers has been a refreshing breeze. The substitution of understanding for rote, practice for drill, and problem solving for getting the answer is directly attributable to the constructivist point of view. Similarly, the infusion of new topics and the use of electronic devices in the classroom breathed new life into the discipline. Together they raised the level of learning to the next rung on Bloom's hierarchy.

After studying the problem-solving characteristics, strategy selection and use, and verification actions of African-American eighth-grade students, Malloy and Jones (1998) found that holistic rather than analytic reasoning was used. More importantly, like good problem solvers of any race, they successfully use strategies, are flexible in approach, verify their actions and outcomes, and recognize and dismiss irrelevant detail.

More generally, "best practices" may be enhanced through multicultural emphasis, and shaped by the disciplines, but these are accidental compared with the shared psychological basis underlying learning and instruction.

TEACHER RESOURCES

A priori teachers are the most important instructional resource. They set the stage for and manage the learning environment. Good teachers may overcome the challenges of scarce resources, but abundant resources will never fill the void created by poorly prepared teachers. Teacher shortages in urban districts mean that a disproportionate number of underprepared individuals are hired and assigned to the classroom. Administrators are justifiably relieved to place fully certified teachers from any background with children rather than conditionally certified laymen. Aware of these conditions, the reform movement is keenly interested in the qualifications of math and science instructors. Data indicates that the vast majority of high school science teachers—and virtually all mathematics teachers—hold certificates in the disciplines. Below high school, the context backgrounds, and therefore, content knowledge in both math and science becomes progressively slimmer. Sadly, this is particularly detrimental to poor minority youngsters as urban middle school teachers increasingly hold elementary certification. At the critical middle school level when students' career paths and ambitions take shape, they lack role models in the classroom. As a consequence of poorly prepared, or misassigned teachers urban, minority children are distanced from high-quality math and science education.

Conditions will probably worsen among ethnically diverse groups whose numbers increase while available role models shy away from the classroom. Inevitably, children's social needs for role models will tug at the academic fabric of the schools because luring certified, minority candidates to urban schools is increasingly problematic.

> The long-term effect of minority under representation in mathematics is magnified because so many mathematics professionals are teachers. During the next decade, 30 percent of public school children, but only five percent of their mathematics teachers, will be minorities. The inescapable fact is that two demographic forces—increasing Black and Hispanic youth in the classroom, decreasing Black and Hispanic graduates in mathematics—will virtually eliminate classroom role models for those students who most need motivation, incentive, and high-quality teaching of mathematics. The under representation of this generation of minorities leads to further under representation in the next, yielding and unending cycle of mathematical poverty. (NRC, 1989, p. 21)

Can America's children maintain their place in the world let alone become the "best" given marginally prepared teachers?

RETROSPECTIVE AND COMMENTARY

Central to this chapter was an exploration of tensions related to the reform movement in MS education. Of particular concern were the historic, strategic, academic, social, and evaluative aspects of this national movement and how they related to inclusion. Two social beacon's—*Science for All Americans*, and *Everybody Counts*—justify and outline the need for change in MS education, present the primary social and academic goals of reform, describe the environment of change and the nature of the academic disciplines. In the process, they identify the stakeholders, the setting for learning, and the instructional style aspired to by the reform movement. In the political rhetoric, our national goal must be to make the U.S. mathematics and science education the leader in the world reform—an Olympics of the mind. However, no platform will be mounted, or national anthem played until a multitiered challenge is mastered:

- Make MS education effective by implementing challenging standards in mathematics and science for all Americans.
- Develop or implement new assessment, instructional and curricula approaches appropriate to the mathematical and scientific needs of the 21st century.
- Improve significantly the mathematical and scientific achievement of students.

These lofty aspirations provided a compass for the last, and arguably the most significant, educational reform movement of the 20th century.

Strategically, the movement joined federal, political interests and funding with professional, discipline based organizations to develop and promulgate sets of standards, plus a process for their attainment. The dynamics of change differed markedly from earlier, major, educational reform movements. From the sense of applications to the real world, integration of content, use of group problem solving and the concept of constructed knowledge the roots of change may be traced to Dewey. Several sharp contrasts exist between this approach and the 1960s curriculum reform. First, the preceding reform movement distanced itself from politics as opposed to the more politically astute strategy that invited and supported state education department participation and ownership. The current approach was to set the stage not write the script for states or local districts to follow. Change is prefaced on the belief that the federal government along with professional organizations can establish the foundation for a national movement through the development and promulgation of academic standards. The NCTM created the standards for mathematics, and the NRC formulated the compromise resulting in the National Science Education Standards. Second, federal money supported the establishment of standards and related testing programs. Scores on authentic instruments indicate areas of success or need within local school districts, occasionally even the building level. In this process, local educational agencies are responsible for making and funding changes in curriculum, or professional development programs needed to meet relevant standards. Third, in the 1960s mathematics and science curricula were considered separately and developed independently. Today's reform links mathematics, science, and technology and is unified in strategy and approach. Fourth, curriculum development during the Cold War era was led by experts in the disciplines whose primary goal was to create future American scientists or mathematicians. To this end, NSF financed the development of supposedly "teacher-proof" national programs but recognized the need for substantial professional development. Today, empowered teachers adapt curriculum to meet state or local standards.

> Perhaps novel in U.S. education is the extensive use of assessment to catalyze educational change. Implementation of standards has been promoted, pushed actually, through assessment. Test items require students to display both knowledge and thought processes, reflect the underlying constructivist philosophy, and stress the use of hands-on curriculum materials and instructional approaches. By sharing test scores through local presses, states prod districts to emphasize material found on examinations.

Inclusion of "all Americans" was and is the movement's greatest social imperative. Reformers insisted on improving the level of instruction and participation for groups who have been traditionally by-passed—women, ethnic minorities, and non-English speakers. Although the clarion call, and intent of MS reform is undeniably inclusive, paradoxes, perhaps insurmountable hurdles, exist that spring from the implementation strategy as well as the nature of the disciplines. Proponents consider standards a measure of expertise that can be used to assess individual accomplishments based on them in a valid, moral way. Because readily identified subgroups such as poor, minority youngsters will have difficulty meeting the standards even at the most basic levels, some critics see the mere establishment of standards as inherently exclusive. In a "bottom line" sense, groups who had difficulty meeting expectations have difficulty meeting standards.

The nature of the disciplines creates a paradox related to multiculturalism. Science and mathematics are different than most areas studied in K–12. Neither discipline is as culturally bound or as culturally influenced as literature, music, and history. On the contrary, mathematics and science have their own cultural manifestation and interactions. Mathematics approaches cultural neutrality because successful mathematical principles have been assimilated into and used by all cultures. Although any gender identification invites a degree of controversy, the intellectual wellspring of the scientific approach to problem solving and its fruits are disproportionately European and male.

Ultimately, education should provide the skills, knowledge, understanding, and attitudes necessary for individuals to enter the mainstream of U.S. economic and political life. Given the explosion in knowledge, center stage must be given to enduring concepts and processes. Fewer topics should be crammed into curricula, and central ideas probed far more deeply than in the past. Skills, drills, and frills are no longer enough.

Instructional techniques implemented to heighten multiculturalism tends to stress sensitivity to other cultures and role models who happen to be Asian, Hispanic, Native American, or African American as opposed to studying science concepts that were generated by one or the other of these groups. Emphasis is on creating cultural links rather than recreating the content of the curriculum.

Of all the areas of inclusion touched by reform, the academic progress — indicated by test scores — made by females is probably the most noteworthy. In the 1960s and 1970s significant differences in the achievement scores between males and females were predictable on indicators such as the Scholastic Aptitude Tests or the National Assessment of Educational Progress (NAEP). Through raised consciousness and expectations, the demand for equal treatment, recognition of career alternatives, and the use of instructional techniques such as cooperative learning, women and men are all but indistinguishable based on their test results on the latest NAEP. As the millenium begins, the gender gap has narrowed dramatically.

Applause for any attempt to foster educational change is invariably muted, and greeted in several predictable ways. Cynics dismiss all "new ideas" as old. A radical minority opposes any change as an attack on the three Rs. Some, searching for answers, welcome any attempts to change school practice because of age-old dissatisfaction with the outcomes of schooling. MS reform has been greeted with such a range of responses. Yet, the politically astute strategy touches almost every classroom in the nation at one level or another. At the most basic level, teachers realize that they must prepare students for a statewide test that is driven directly or indirectly by national standards. More altruistic teachers try to create a challenging, active learning environment where each child can meet the standards at a high level.

REFERENCES

American Association for the Advancement of Science (AAAS). (1990). *Science for all Americans*. New York: Oxford University Press

American Association for the Advancement of Science (AAAS). (1993). *Benchmarks for science literacy*. New York: Oxford University Press.

Darling-Hammond, L. (1993). Reframing the school reform agenda. *Phi Delta Kappan, 74*(10), 753-761.

Feng, J. (1994). Asian American children: What teachers should know. Columbus, OH: ERIC Clearinghouse on Elementary and Early Childhood Education. [ENC-009581]

Gallard, A.J. (1992). Creating a multicultural learning environment in science classrooms. *Journal of Research in Science Teaching, 29*.

Goodman, J. (1995). Change without difference: School restructuring in historical perspective. *Harvard Educational Review, 65*, 1.

Hiebert, J. (1999). Relationships between research and the NCTM standards. *Journal of Research in Mathematics Education, 30*(1), 3.

Malloy, C.E., & Jones, M.G. (1998). An investigation of African American students' mathematical problem solving. *Journal of Research in Mathematics Education, 29*(2), 143.

National Assessment Governing Board. (1997). *National Assessment of Educational Progress 1996v Science Performance Standards*. Washington, DC: U.S. Department of Education.

National Commission on Excellence in Education. (1983). *A nation at risk*. Washington, DC: U.S. Department of Education.

National Education Goals Panel. (1997). *Goals Report Summary Mathematics and Science Achievement for the 21st Century*. Washington, DC . (http://www.negp .gov).

National Research Council. (1989). *Everybody counts: A report to the nation on the future of mathematics education*. Washington, DC: National Academy Press.

National Research Council. (1990). *National Science Education Standards*. Washington, DC: National Academy Press.

Ross, A. (Ed.). (1996). *Science wars*. Durham, NC: Duke University Press.

Schmidt, W.H., McKnight, C.C., & Raizen, S.A. (1999). *A splintered vision: An investigation of U.S. science and mathematics education*. East Lansing, MI: U.S. National Research Center, Michigan State University.

Siegel, H. (1995). What price inclusion? *Teachers College Record, 97*, 6-31. http://www.ed.uiuc.edu/eps/pes-yearbook/95_docs/siegel.html.

Simon, M.A. (1995). Reconstructing mathematics pedagogy from a constructivist perspective. *Journal for Research in Mathematics Education, 26*, 114.

U.S. Department of Education. (1997). *Mathematics equals opportunity*. Washington, DC: U.S. Government Printing

7

Educational Choice and the Politics of Inclusion

A True Story

Robert Palestini

Saint Joseph's University

In my life before higher education, I was superintendent of a large urban Catholic school system. With more than 160,000 students, it was one of the largest school systems in the nation. Like many U.S. urban school systems, both public and nonpublic, it was in a state of decline. *Rightsizing* was the "name of the game."

I found myself in the all too familiar position of having to close or merge a number of schools, not because they were not academically effective, but because they were not financially viable. What pained me the most about closing these schools was that, more often than not, the students in them had been outperforming their public school counterparts only a block or two away, as well as in other parochial schools in the system.

Invariably, after their schools were closed, the great majority of these students were destined to complete their education in a school setting that by all standard measures was inferior to the one where they had been. These families, who were virtually all non-Catholic minorities, deserved better. They deserved better because they were human beings, but also because they had made monumental sacrifices to afford their children the education that they believed best met their needs.

Despite many of them being on welfare, they had somehow adjusted their priorities to be able to pay the $1,200 annual tuition charged by these schools. And despite living in deplorable conditions and enduring what Kozol (1991) described as the "savage inequalities" of urban life, they somehow had the intuitive judgment to choose the school that they perceived best met their children's educational needs, even if it required financial sacrifices.

I relate this story so that my biases are known. Nonetheless, I still believe strongly that something new and different needs to be done to mitigate these injustices. Perhaps providing educational choice through tuition vouchers may be a way to address these injustices, and in the process, improve all aspects of American education; that is to say, in my mind at least, this is not an issue of public versus nonpublic. Nor is it an indictment of public schools. The issue of school choice transcends public versus nonpublic; it is an issue of being truly democratic and providing the best available education to all of our young people, no matter the setting. In some cases, it will be a public school. In others, it may be a parochial school. And, in still others, it may be a private school, a for-profit school, or a charter school. Nonetheless, we need to find a way to better empower parents, the child's first teachers, to make the decision as to what type of schooling best meets their children's needs. What follows is an exploration of possible ways of doing so; this despite those who would take issue with this cause.

INTRODUCTION

Economic inequality in the United States is growing, and it threatens to tear the heart out of our civil society. Given the faith Americans have always placed in education as an engine of material and cultural progress, schools will inevitably be asked to play an ethical role in reversing this destructive trend (Molnar, 1997).

This chapter examines the role of educators in providing an opportunity in schools and in classrooms for all children to succeed—not just the White children, not just the brightest children, not only the well-behaved students, or the socioeconomically advantaged students, but all students. *Inclusion*, as defined in this text, is the egalitarian and critical view that there is an ethical responsibility on the part of educators to provide literally all young people with real and equal access to a quality education. Anything else becomes the politics of exclusion.

Despite the many arguments that diminish the rationale behind school choice, I suggest that one important way of ensuring that all children have the opportunity to achieve is for each state to consider implementing a school choice program funded by educational tuition vouchers. I know that a notion such as this is considered to be heresy by many in the so-called "public school establishment." Many of its opponents characterize school choice as the strategy of neo-conservatives to exploit the dissatisfaction of poor, predominantly minority parents who have been left behind by our economy in order to achieve the goal of creating a publicly funded private school system free of public control and oversight. If achieved, they say, this alternative system will inevitably reproduce and legally sanction the doctrine of "separate but equal" on a grand scale, with the primary beneficiaries being middle- and upper middle-class families. In other words, the politics of private school choice now resembles a high-stakes version of the old "bait and switch" scam (Molnar, Farrell, Johnson, & Sapp, 1997). Unfortunately, such ad hominum, strident, and inflammatory arguments are too often the knee-jerk reactions of many of the school choice protagonists.

I venture to say that most members of the public school establishment, as well as many academics (some in this book), therefore, would consider voucher plans to be exclusionary, rather than inclusionary, and would ultimately render the public schools as the educators of the lowest strata of our society. Such a view defies our limited experience with educational vouchers. The reality is that a well-crafted system of educational vouchers, awarded according to economic need and physical and mental disability, could serve as a vehicle for inclusion that would enable many of the most underserved students in our society to choose a school that they and their parents consider to be superior. And, because of the introduction of some healthy competition, all schools, including the public schools, may benefit.

The suggested voucher plan would be limited to a relatively small group of young people whose families are economically disadvantaged or who have a child with a physical or mental disability. Thus, such a plan would not have a significant negative impact on public school enrollment. The Milwaukee and the Cleveland plans come immediately to mind as examples of how such a system could work, although none of these models includes vouchers for those who have physical and/or mental disabilities. The outcomes of both the Milwaukee and Cleveland voucher plans have been positive, and neither city has experienced a significant decline in public school enrollment, or any of the other Armageddon-like consequences that many have predicted (Parry, 1997). Furthermore, it is interesting to note that until recently, the great majority of the countries in the world that have government dollars going exclusively to public or state schools were communist, and other types of dictatorships, whereas the great majority of the democratic countries in the world provide government aid to a variety of schools, including private schools (Coleman & Hoeffer, 1987). I believe that it is time to reconsider our current monolithic paradigm whereby only public schools are funded through taxpayers' dollars.

In exploring this topic, I consider three perspectives: the market economy, the liberal tradition, and the critical pedagogy models. The market-driven model is most concerned with efficiency of operation. These theorists might ask, "How can we deliver education and achieve the 'biggest bang for the buck?'" Those in the liberal tradition are concerned with equality. They might ask, "How can we assure that every student has an equal opportunity to achieve?" The critical pedagogues are concerned with social justice and inclusion. They might ask, "How can we structure our educational systems so that the least privileged and the least powerful are not marginalized?"

THE THEORETICAL DEVELOPMENT OF SCHOOL CHOICE

Assuming some level of government financing, the school choice issue comes down to this: Should students be assigned to schools based on politically established criteria, or should they be able to choose the schools they will attend? Any answer must contain qualifications and caveats. The following is a review of several influential school choice proposals and the accompanying rationales given for greater reliance on markets and democratic principles for providing education. In my conclusions, I relate my recommendations and observations to one or more of these theories or rationales.

THE MARKET ECONOMY MODEL

Friedman's (1955) market economy voucher model has been enormously influential (Lamdin, 1997). The market economy model posits that education should be allowed to be subjected to the exigencies of supply and demand just as most other products and services are in a capitalistic country. Friedman reasoned that, in a society based on voluntary cooperation, all individuals must have a basic level of education. Friedman admitted that it is difficult to determine precisely where the public benefits of education stop and the private benefits begin. Yet, because there is a public benefit to education, he argued that some public action should be taken to ensure the adequate education of all members of society. Because of noncompliance problems, Friedman said this action must involve more than setting school attendance rules. Hence, he proposed that subsidies be provided to those families who could not cover the costs of educating their children (Goldhaber, 1997).

Friedman (1955) next noted that although government financing and provision of education are typically combined, they could and should be separated. The financing function should be achieved by giving subsidies to families through educational vouchers to purchase a specified minimum amount of education per child per year, if spent on approved educational services. Friedman suggested that parents be free to spend the voucher amount and any additional amount on the school of their choice. Furthermore, education could be supplied by a range of organizations, including for-profit firms and nonprofit institutions. The government's role would be restricted to upholding minimum standards, including, perhaps, the teaching of some minimum common content.

Having made this proposal, Freidman (1955) defended it against potential criticisms. Where decentralized decision making could lead to the same outcome as centralized decision making, Friedman argued that the decentralized route should be taken for two reasons. First, the use of collective decision making tends to strain the social cohesion essential for a stable society. Second, government decision making requires that once decisions are made, people must conform to them, even if they disagree. As well as potentially engendering ill feeling, this need to conform also stifles innovation. Friedman argued that a system of education vouchers would allow greater individual decision making and would create competition among educational institutions, a powerful force for promoting innovative schooling practices.

Friedman's proposal was rather simple. Rather than elaborate on the details of such an approach, he chose to show that many arguments against it can just as easily be made against the present system of schooling. For example, Friedman argued that it is disingenuous to claim that vouchers will exacerbate class distinction. In looking at the present organization of education in society, we find that there is much stratification, even when schooling is produced primarily in the public sector. Thus, Friedman (1962) claimed:

> Under present arrangements, stratification of residential areas effectively restricts the intermingling of children from decidedly different backgrounds. In addition parents are not now prevented from sending their children to private schools. Only a highly limited class can or does do so, parochial schools aside, thus producing further stratification. (p. 127)

Friedman (1955) concluded that the present school system appears to promote inequality, and he saw this as a serious problem in that it makes it all the harder for the exceptional few who are the hope of the future to rise above the poverty of their initial state.

THE LIBERAL TRADITION

A number of educational theorists are uncomfortable with Friedman's model because their observations were that when individuals are left to their own devices in determining their behavior, often, prejudices and discrimination surface. Those theorists in the liberal tradition were concerned about equal opportunity and equity of treatment.

The liberal tradition started with sociologist Christopher Jencks, who suggested that private schools could help to remedy educational problems in the inner city. A veteran teacher, Mario Fantini, wrote a book on alternative public schools in which he argued for the use of vouchers within the public school system. Education academics John Coons and Stephen Sugarman (1978) argued for the use of vouchers to address equity concerns.

Jencks (1966) was motivated by the perilous state of inner-city public schools. In his view, the problems facing these schools originated from the overly bureaucratic nature of the systems they operated within and the low pay levels of teachers and administrators. In combination, Jencks argued, this has led to the creation of a system of education whose first axiom is that everyone, on every level, is incompetent and irresponsible. As a result, innovative ideas are very unlikely to emerge from the lower ranks in the hierarchy and top–down reforms become difficult to implement.

In developing his argument, Jencks suggested that government-financed education vouchers, or tuition grants, combined with private-school provision, would have two major benefits. First, private control would make it possible to attack management problems. Second, the use of tuition grants would put an end to neighborhood schools. Jencks believed that education involves interacting with others from a variety of socioeconomic backgrounds. However, the neighborhood schools with their specified attendance zones prevent this sort of mixing. Jencks admitted that these actions would destroy the public school system. In response to this, Jencks (cited in Lamdin & Mintrom) said,

> we must not allow the memory of past achievements to blind us to present failures. (p. 211)

Having developed this theoretical justification for school choice, in association with his colleagues from the Center for the Study of Public Policy at Harvard, Jencks went on to design a voucher system to transform inner-city schooling. This work led to the Alum Rock, California experiment, which is discussed later. In contrast to Friedman's relatively simple, straightforward voucher plan, Jencks' plan was very complex. In an effort in ensure equal opportunity and equity, Jencks' plan contained rules for how applicants could choose their schools, how schools could choose their applicants and how lottery systems would operate in cases of oversubscription.

Another theorist is the liberal tradition is Mario Fantini (1973). Fantini's theoretical contribution extended discussion of the ways that education vouchers could promote innovations. He contrasted himself with Friedman and Jencks by arguing that the public school system could reform itself and ensure equal opportunity and equity. Fantini called for an "internal voucher" that would allow real alternatives to emerge in the public school system. Fantini did not want vouchers to apply to nonpublic schools for fear that low-quality schools would emerge. The Minnesota voucher plan, which is discussed later, operationalized many of Fantini's principles.

Fantini's model was designed to give parents, students, and teachers choice among alternative types of schools. He suggested a "house" concept, whereby schools would be subdivided into houses for science, foreign languages, humanities, and so on, so that greater individual attention could be given. According to some, Fantini stands alone in making an education-inspired case for school choice (Lamdin & Mintrom, 1997). Although his work received a wide amount of interest within education circles at the time it was published, Fantini is rarely cited in contemporary debates. But his ideas influenced individuals who have become important voices in the school choice debate.

Also in the liberal tradition, Coons and Sugarman (1978) took as their starting point the observation that a just society must provide the formal portion of a child's education. They placed primary emphasis on promoting educational equity. This made their plan for school choice become complicated because of the substantial differences in income among individuals in American society. According to Coons and Sugarman, educational vouchers needed to differ in amount depending on family income and on the tuition charges at the chosen school. Unlike previous theoretical work on school choice approaches, this approach required extensive data on family size and income in order to be implemented. Thus, in an effort to ensure equity, the process can become administratively cumbersome.

In 1990, The Brookings Institute published John Chubb and Terry Moe's (1990) book, *Politics, Markets, and America's Schools,* a book central to recent school choice debates. In it they combined the market economy theory with that of the liberal tradition. They considered their voucher rationale to be implemented in the Harlem District 4 experiment, which is discussed in more detail later.

Chubb and Moe, both political scientists, took as their starting point the observation that, by most accounts the American education system is not working well. They took an organizational development approach to analyzing the problem and concluded that the institutional arrangements that have evolved in public schools make them unresponsive and ineffective.

In their empirical work, Chubb and Moe built on the finding of James Coleman (Coleman & Hoffers, 1987) that school autonomy was the single most important element in the success of schools in academic achievement. Based on these findings, Chubb and Moe asserted that bureaucracy is unambiguously problematic for school organization. But bureaucracy is an essential for democratic control. Therefore, Chubb and Moe concluded that because the institutions of democratic control work systematically and powerfully to discourage school autonomy, in turn they discourage school effectiveness. If public schools are to become more effective, the institutions that control them must be changed. To improve U.S. schools, they proposed a new system eliminating centralized bureaucracies and vesting authority directly in the hands of schools, parents, and students.

THE CRITICAL PEDAGOGY PERSPECTIVE

The critical pedagogy perspective grows out of strongly held beliefs that schooling cannot be separated from the social context within which it takes place. Thus, a discourse on ethics, the distribution of power, and the plight of the underserved must be included in any debate on how education should be delivered (Gintis, 1989). Critical pedagogists decry the current heavy emphasis on testing to assess academic achievement. Thus, any notion of educational choice that develops out of a disparity of test scores between public and nonpublic school students is very problematic. Those espousing this perspective would posit that, in this context, school choice is organized and developed according to the logic and imperatives of the marketplace. Ignoring the primacy of the social, choice appeals to the logic of the market place, competitiveness, individualism, and achievement. Although these attributes might sound plausible as fundamental elements in the logic of educational reform, they, in fact, are used by neo-conservatives, like Friedman, to develop a notion of educational leadership that undermines the responsibility of public service, to rupture the relationship between schools and the community, and to divert educators from improving education in all schools (Buchanan, Tollison, & Tulloch, 1980).

These theorists are also alarmed that the new educational reform movements, including school choice, refuse to develop a deeper critical moral discourse. More specifically, missing from the current neo-conservative emphasis on educational reform is a discourse that can illuminate what administrators, teachers, and other cultural workers actually do in terms of the underlying principles and values that structure the stories, visions, and experiences that inform school and classroom practices. Accountability in this discourse offers few insights into how schools should prepare students to push against the oppressive boundaries of gender, class, race, and age domination. Nor does such a language provide the conditions for students to interrogate how questions and matters concerning the curriculum are really struggles concerning issues of self-identity, culture, power, and history. In effect, the crisis of authority is grounded in a refusal to address how particular forms of authority are secured and legitimized at the expense of cultural democracy, critical citizenship, and basic human rights. Refusing to interrogate the values that not only frame how authority is constructed but also define leadership as a political and pedagogical practice, neo-conservative educational reformers end up subordinating the discourse of ethics to the rules of management and efficiency.

Despite these concerns, however, there are critical pedagogy theorists who posit that, if one could devise a well-crafted choice plan that takes into consideration the aforementioned concerns, it could be effective. Herbert Gintis (1996), a neo-Marxist, is one such theorist. He contended that the analysis of the competitive delivery of educational services has often been couched in terms of an opposition between government regulation and the free market. However, the regulation and markets may be complementary institutions that under appropriate conditions interact as a context for cost-effective egalitarian and socially accountable education. The government must provide some services on a monopolistic basis because competitive delivery of these services may be excessively costly. Tax collection, police protection, national defense, and other regulatory agencies are examples. In each case, one could make a compelling argument that competitive delivery would not be effective. In the case of education, however, it would be more difficult to make such a compelling argument. In fact, unless there are structural forces prohibiting the emergence of effective regulation, or the costs of efficient regulation are excessively high, competitive delivery of educational services should better meet the private needs of parents and children, while fulfilling the educational systems traditional social functions as well (see Coleman, Hoffer, & Kilgore, 1982).

Gintis maintained that the public has certain expectations of schools: reading, writing, history, math, and science, punctuality, and self-discipline. If parents are dissatisfied with the results of what they are getting, it would be advantageous to them to be able to leverage their dissatisfaction in support of change, by using the threat of "taking their business elsewhere." The existing public school establishment disempowers parents by obliging them to utilize a Byzantine governance system to effect change. The competitive delivery of educational services, properly funded and regulated, might succeed in expediting and circumventing this cumbersome process.

Educators, on the other hand, have higher expectations for education. In addition to reading, writing, and arithmetic, they expect promotion of equality and tolerance, teaching artistic, aesthetic and spiritual values, and creating community. The idea that these ideals can be promoted in a marketplace model is repugnant to many, but need not be the case if the school choice program is properly crafted. The choice of educational goals can still be debated in the political arena, and the results could be implemented through the proper choice of policy tools. They would be codified in the rules for funding and accrediting schools. The use of the market is in this sense an "instrument" of rather than an "alternative to" democratic policy-making (Downs, 1951).

A CASE FOR SCHOOL CHOICE

The rather widespread and growing appeal of school choice may be attributed to several key factors (Goldhaber, 1997). First, on average, nonpublic school students outperform their public school counterparts in terms of standardized achievement test scores, graduation rates, and the probability of attending college (Gollner, 1993). Proponents of school choice argue that these results can be explained by the greater efficiency of nonpublic schools, which do not have the bloated bureaucracy and rigid set of policies that impede good teaching and learning and make public schools less effective. However, an alternative explanation is that differences in performance between students in public and nonpublic schools can be explained by differences in school resources or in the backgrounds of students (Berliner & Biddle, 1995). For instance, nonpublic school students tend to come from better educated families with above average incomes. It seems likely, opponents of school choice argue, that these factors would contribute to a good educational environment in the home. Still, the fact that private school students generally outperform their public school counterparts lends credence to the notion that nonpublic schools are doing a better job of educating students than are public schools.

Second, vouchers would give more control over educational decisions to parents. When more control is yielded to the consumers of education, those who presumably have the best knowledge of the educational needs and desires of the children are allowed to use that knowledge in selecting a school. Because most parents believe that they know what is best for their children, it is difficult, politically, to argue against this position.

Finally, and probably most important, public schools are commonly perceived to be in such a sorry state that many people are willing to try any program that might help improve them (Odden & Massy, 1992). It is widely reported that U.S. children consistently rank lower than those of many other industrialized countries on international tests in mathematics and science (Hanushek, 1996). And, at the same time as these reports have proliferated, expenditures for education in the United States have increased greatly. Total K–12 expenditures per pupil, in real current dollars, increased 35% in the 1970s and 33% in the 1980s (Goldhaber & Brewer, 1997). Throwing money at the problem seems not to have led to any clear improvements (Hedges, Laine, & Greenwald, 1994). Quite simply, many people have become fed up with the current system.

A CASE AGAINST SCHOOL CHOICE

The major concern of those who oppose school choice is the potential for inequities in a voucher program. The danger of a voucher plan is that there could be a significant movement of students from public to private schools, resulting in a loss of tax support and lower per-pupil expenditures in public schools. Vouchers would probably cover only a portion of tuition at many private schools. For instance, the recent California amendment offered a voucher worth $2,600, a figure less than half the statewide average for private school tuition. Thus, even under a voucher plan the majority of private schools would continue to attract students from families with above average incomes and would remain out of reach for many lower income families. If this were to happen, public schools could end up becoming "dumping grounds" for disadvantaged students (Goldhaber, 1997).

Parents might also choose their children's schools for the wrong reasons. For school choice to lead to improvements, the competition between schools should be based on educational quality. However, past evidence provided by Clotfelter (1976) and new evidence that is cited later suggest that, independent of the quality of the school, the racial composition of a school may be an important factor in parental decisions to send their children to private schools. Hence, choice could lead to greater segregation without improving overall educational outcomes. Vouchers may also open the door for discrimination because private schools are not required by law to accept all students who apply for admission. Finally, some people simply object to school choice because it is offered as a false panacea that will distract attention from the real problems of funding and equity that now exist in the public schools.

EMPIRICAL EVIDENCE

We can distinguish two types of empirical evidence that bear on the school choice debate: indirect and direct evidence. The indirect evidence comes from research done in situations similar to school choice experiments, but not on the actual school districts where school choice has taken place. Generally, this research measures achievement levels of students in public versus private schools. The direct evidence comes from the relatively few school choice experiments that have been implemented in the United States. How these data are interpreted or valued depends on one's theoretical perspective.

INDIRECT EMPIRICAL EVIDENCE

Studies of the achievement differences between students at public and private schools are numerous. These data would make a compelling argument to many in the market economy school and to some in the liberal tradition, whereas critical pedagogues would not be impressed. Nonetheless, several studies find that private schools are more effective than public schools (see Coleman & Hoffer, 1987). These studies were controversial and generated questions regarding problems such as the focus on standardized test scores as the performance measure, the sensitivity of results to the choice of independent variables, results that were statistically significant but perhaps not substantively significant and, perhaps most important, the problem of selection bias.

Recent contributors to the study of public versus private school performance are aware of these problems and have addressed some or all of them. Evans and Schwab (1996) examine the *High School and Beyond* data, but focus on the probability of finishing high school and entering higher education rather than on gains in test scores. With other factors being held constant, Catholic school students have a 12% higher probability of finishing high school and a 14% higher probability of entering higher education than do public school students. Sander (1996) found that Catholic grade schools produce higher vocabulary, mathematics, and reading scores, but the same science scores as public schools. Curiously, however, this positive impact of Catholic schools is driven by non-Catholic students in Catholic schools. Goldhaber (1997) found that private schools do not use resources more efficiently to produce higher test scores than public schools. Rather, the difference in test scores in favor of private schools is due to characteristics of the students and the schools' resources. Toma (1996) took advantage of the variety of financing and provision combinations observed internationally to examine their impact on a standardized mathematics examination. She found that in the United States, Belgium, and New Zealand, the private schools outperformed the public schools. No difference was found in Canada or France. Dingdon (1997) examined data from India and reported that the privately funded schools outperformed both the publicly funded schools and the publicly funded and regulated, but nominally private, schools on reading and mathematics test. Neal (1997) examines graduation rate, rates of advancement to postsecondary education and wages, and finds that the superior performance by Catholic schools is evident primarily for urban minority students. He attributes this difference to the low quality of the public alternative. In summary, the weight of evidence in the newer set of studies suggest superior performance in private schools (see Lamdin, 1997).

Private schools are usually shown to be less costly than public schools. For example, Lott (1990) reports that public school teachers are paid 20% more than their private school counterparts, and that operating expenditures of public schools exceed those of private schools by 80%. Based on another source (Lott, 1993), public school teachers are paid 50% more than private school teachers. Tuition data provide a convenient estimate of the cost of operating a private school. Recent average tuition figures are $2138 for elementary schools, $4578 for secondary schools, $4266 for combined schools, and an overall average of approximately $5000 for districts with 20,000 or more students (Lamdin, 1997). Levin (Levin & Kelley, 1994), however, is circumspect about private and public school cost comparisons. One reason for this is that differences in the service mix increase the relative cost of public schools. Tuition may not include costs that are included in public school costs. These might include textbooks and supplies, transportation, and additional fees for specialized services. Also, tuition underestimates costs insofar as contributions and endowments are used to reduce tuition (Lamdin, 1997). Hoxby reports that 56% of Catholic elementary school income and 19% of secondary school income are from these sources.

DIRECT EMPIRICAL EVIDENCE

The history of tentative, geographically limited steps toward school choice in the United States began in the 1970s, with the Alum Rock, California voucher demonstration. As noted earlier, this experiment operationalized Jencks' liberal tradition voucher theory. Parents in voucher school attendance areas were allowed to choose among several "minischools," alternative educational programs organized within schools, and, during the 5 years of the experiment the number of programs increased from 22 in 6 schools to 51 in 14 schools. These parents were allowed to choose among programs in any voucher school; parents and students in nonvoucher school areas were treated as controls. For voucher participants, free transportation was provided to non-neighborhood schools, and transfers were permitted during the year. Students who attended in the past or who had siblings enrolled in a given school were granted preferential access. And a lottery was used to assign admissions to over subscribed programs (Capell, 1976).

Given that it was an experiment, the Alum Rock voucher plan was studied using a systematic, across-time research strategy. Surveys administered during the demonstration showed that voucher parents were consistently more knowledgeable about program options, transportation and transfer rights than those who did not participate. Parents with children in voucher schools were more satisfied with their schools than in the past. Parental appreciation may have followed from the substance of the new programs or simply from being offered a choice, but whatever the reason the opportunity to choose seems to have been welcomed (Weiler, 1977).

Although closely monitored, the results of the Alum Rock experiment were mixed in terms of student performance and provided no basis for supporting or criticizing voucher initiatives. Results from the California state testing program showed a decline in voucher-student reading scores compared with their own age-adjusted performance prior to the experiment. Scores also dropped in comparison to the scores of students in nonvoucher schools. However, results from the metropolitan achievement test (MAT) showed that voucher-students' scores increased about as much as those of students in Alum Rock Title I schools (i.e., schools eligible for federal funding to help poor children) who received the same test. Other evidence regarding student behavior was more positive. Unexcused absence rates dropped slightly for voucher-school students during the demonstration and student attitudes toward school also appeared to improve (see Lamdin, 1997).

Following the Alum Rock experiment, many other school districts experimented with school choice schemes, frequently relying on a small number of alternative schools and magnet schools to break the usual procedures for matching students with schools. But it would be incorrect to conclude much from this research. Access to these specialty programs and magnet schools is often highly competitive and restrictive. An important exception, however, is District 4, located in the Harlem area of New York City.

Another voucher program in the liberal tradition, the factors shaping the District 4 of today can be traced back to the late 1960s. Then, the administration of New York City's public school system was decentralized to allow for greater local control. In 1972, the district consisted of 22 schools. But during the late 1970s and 1980s, about 30 alternative schools were developed so that more than 50 schools now exist. After 1982, all families of incoming seventh graders had the opportunity to choose a school. There have been no systematic studies of the effects of school choice in District 4, although some analyses have been conducted and the results have been widely discussed (see Heneg, 1994). In the early 1970s, the district was ranked the lowest in the City for mathematics and reading scores. Although some controversy surrounds test score measures, student performance in the district appears to be significantly improved over performance in the district before changes started being made in the mid-1970s. Schools in District 4 also seem to enjoy greater levels of parental involvement than schools in districts with less well-developed choice programs (Schneider, Teske, Marscall,

Mintrom, & Rooch, 1996). Thus, District 4 has received much critical acclaim from outside observers. For instance, Chubb and Moe (1990), both liberal theorists, have suggested that "If there is a single school district in the country that deserves to be held up as a model for all others, it is East Harlem" (p. 82).

Since the late 1980s, there have been many proposals for greater use of publicly funded vouchers. All but two of these proposals had been defeated until school choice was approved in Milwaukee (1994) and Cleveland (1996). The Milwaukee parental choice program probably comes closest to approximating the voucher model that Friedman had in mind, although it is not nearly as universal as he envisioned. Because these plans are aimed primarily at urban student populations, they would also possess many of the characteristics espoused by theorists in the liberal tradition and the critical pedagogues.

The program provides an opportunity for students meeting specific criteria to opt out of the Milwaukee Public Schools and attend private schools in the city. Recently, this opportunity was extended to religiously affiliated nonpublic schools. Students must come from households with income less than 1.75 times the poverty level. They may not have been in private schools or in a school district other than the Milwaukee school district in the previous year. In selecting students, the schools cannot discriminate on the basis of race, religion, gender, prior achievement, or prior behavioral records. If oversubscribed, selection must be made randomly. Furthermore, choice students can make up a maximum of 49% of the student body. No more than 1% of the students can enroll in a given year. The choice students receive the state's contribution to the cost per student to carry with them to the private school.

The Milwaukee parental choice program has been evaluated by political scientist John Witte (1992) and his associates at the University of Wisconsin at Madison. Over the course of a 5-year study, Witte traced five outcome measures: achievement test results, attendance data, parental attitudes, parental involvement, and attrition from the program.

To analyze achievement test results, Witte matched students in the choice program with a random sample of students from low-income households enrolled in the Milwaukee public schools. He then performed cohort tests as well as analyses of the change scores of the test performance of individual students. As a preliminary point, Witte observed that the students coming into the choice program were clearly behind the average Milwaukee public school students and were also behind a large random sample of low-income students. From the cohort tests, which do not report the same students from year to year, Witte concluded that, in reading and mathematics, there was no significant difference between choice students and public school students.

However, in the areas of attendance, parental involvement, and parental attitudes, Witte found a significant difference in favor of the choice schools, which would appeal to the liberal and critical pedagogy theorists. In summary, then, his study demonstrated that there was improvement at the choice schools in nonacademic areas, but not in the academic areas studied, which disappoints the liberal tradition theorists. But, as market economy theorists are quick to point out, even though both student samples achieved at the same rate, the choice group did so at a significantly lower cost to the taxpayer.

THE MINNESOTA CHOICE PLAN

In 1987, Minnesota introduced a statewide public school-only choice plan, allowing students to attend any school district, subject to space limitation and adherence to desegregation plans. The Minnesota plan was developed in the liberal tradition, especially influenced by Fantini's principles. Although some analysis has been undertaken, there has been no systematic effort to evaluate the Minnesota initiative by making comparisons across experimental and control groups of students and parents. Thus, no information is available on the changes in individual student academic performance that might have occurred as a result of exercising school choice. During the 1989-1990 school year, however, Tenbusch (1993) conducted a survey of parents who had exercised their choice option and those who had not. He found parents to be "active" enrollment decision makers, regardless of whether they chose their local schools or exercised their choice option. He also found that parents who exercised the choice option tended to be more highly educated than those who did not, and that they tended to have more influence than others with school administrators. Delaney (1995) analyzed the reasons why parents of gifted and talented children exercised the choice option in Minnesota. He concluded that the option is used primarily because they anticipated that their children's needs would be better met and their children would receive more personal attention in the choice schools. Law (1994) reported similar results from a more limited study. Ysseldyke (1994) found that parents of students with disabilities who exercised their choice option also did so because they anticipated that their children's needs would be better met and their children would receive more personal attention in the transfer schools. Analyzing aggregate statistics, Colopy and Tarr (1994) concluded that use of the enrollment option increased with time, and that minority students and families use school choice at the same rate as White students and families. The authors also found that use of open enrollment is more likely in smaller districts, suburban and rural districts and higher poverty districts. These findings are particularly appealing to the liberal and critical pedagogy theorists.

In a survey of school principals, Tenbusch and Garet (1993) found that open enrollment stimulated changes in curricula and support services in schools, and promoted more parent and teacher involvement in school planning and decision making. It also increased the ethnic and cultural diversity of schools. Funkhouser and Colopy (1994) reported findings from interviews with school administrators in districts that had lost the most number of students through open enrollment and set of comparison districts. They found that districts losing large numbers of students were more likely to take steps to attract students and to discourage others from leaving than districts that had few losses and few gains and those districts that had net gains in students. Once again, these data dismiss some of the objections of opponents of school choice and bolster the case of the liberal theorists and critical pedagogues.

The Minnesota open enrollment plan has proven to be an influential policy innovation. Since 1987, more than 40 state legislatures have considered a similar form of school choice, and variations of the Minnesota approach have been adopted by at least 18 other states. Although it is true that the Minnesota approach seems a pale shadow of the plans proposed by Friedman and Chubb and Moe, it is important to recognize that, in combination, the various choice approaches now operating in the state are changing the way that public education is delivered. Furthermore, these approaches raise important questions for parents, such as whether to exercise their choice options and what schools to consider if they are making a choice. Although Minnesota has had the longest statewide experience of school choice, and although it has been the focus of considerable research and media attention, many important questions about school choice remain to be addressed using evidence from this state. For example, longitudinal research designs could be used to explore the long-term behavior and attitudes of parents and students making use of the open enrollment option, compared with those who do not. Similar designs could also be used to explore the short-term changes that schools make as a consequence of losing or attracting students and the longer term sustainability of these changes. Studies could also explore whether open enrollment has led to a decline in the use of private school as a means of avoiding local public schools.

NEW INDIRECT EMPIRICAL EVIDENCE

There are a number of educational voucher programs now being implemented, including those in Cleveland, Arizona and, most recently, in the state of Florida. However, these plans are too recent for any direct empirical evidence worth noting to be cited.

Although not directly involving school choice students, Goldhaber (1997), a research analyst with the CNA Corporation, recently conducted a related study that may be helpful in assessing the viability of school choice programs. The underlying assumptions made by many of those who support school choice are: (a) nonpublic schools are more efficient than public schools, (b) parents can distinguish between schools of differing quality, and (c) parents will select schools that perform well. In 1997, Goldhaber completed a study of a nationwide sample of public and private high school students, using data drawn from the National Educational Longitudinal Study (NELS) of 1988, which addresses these issues. He found the evidence mixed with regard to these hypotheses.

The NELS data set is based on a survey conducted by the National Center for Education Statistics (NCES). NCES sampled more than 20,000 eighth graders nationwide, many of whom were surveyed again in the 10th and 12th grades. NELS includes teacher, administrator, parent, and student responses on a variety of survey questions. At several points, NELS administered standardized tests in math, reading, history, and science. Additionally, NELS is unique in that it allows students to be linked directly to their particular classes and teachers. For example, it is possible to determine the actual class size for a particular student rather than just an aggregate measure such as the average pupil–teacher ratio in the school, which is typically the case in other data sets.

In the sample for this study, Goldhaber (1997) drew schoolteacher and class information from the NELS first follow-up survey (1990) and student and family background variables from both the base year (1988) survey and the first follow-up. He focused on achievement of the 10th-grade reading and mathematics standardized tests. The main sample consists of 3,347 Grade 10 students, of whom 451 were in private schools. The reading/English sample consisted of 3,190 students, of whom 399 attended private schools. Students in private schools tend to come from families with better educated parents who have substantially higher incomes than those in the public school sample. Additionally, the parents of private school children already demonstrated an interest in their children's education by choosing to pay for nonpublic schooling.

On average, the private school students outscored their public school counterparts by 7.5 points on the 10th-grade test in mathematics and by 3.8 points on the reading test (see Hanushek, 1996). However, the fact that the parents have consciously chosen private schools brings up an important statistical problem in trying to determine how effective private schools are relative to public schools. Known as *selection bias*, this phenomenon may occur when there are important unobservable characteristics of students that influence achievement and are systematically related to the school sector in which the student is enrolled. These characteristics might include student motivation or the educational environment of the home. Selection bias can easily have come into play in this study, and may have accounted for much of the differences observed (see Gill & Michael, 1992).

In Goldhaber's analysis, he estimated four models of educational achievement based on standardized math and reading tests in public and private schools (see Berliner & Biddle, 1995). These achievement models employ an education production function methodology, in which achievement in Grade 10 is modeled as a function of Grade 8 achievement, student and family background variables, schooling variable, and correction for selection bias (see Hedges et al., 1994).

The results of these achievement models was used to answer questions about the relative efficiency of public schools as opposed to nonpublic schools. If the arguments for the greater efficiency of private schools are accurate, we should observe a higher return on schooling resources in the private sector than in the public sector. Put another way, we might find that a teacher teaching a given set of students in the private sector would be more effective than that same teacher teaching the same set of students in a public school with comparable resources. Statistical tests fail to confirm this hypothesis. In fact, "corrected differentials"—which show what a given student would have achieved in 10th grade had he or she been attending a school in the alternative sector, and brought all schooling characteristics along—show that much of the raw mean difference between sectors disappears when a comparison is made between students of equal ability who have teachers and classmates with similar characteristics (see Goldhaber & Brewer, 1997). Controlling for differences in individuals, families, and schooling resources, Goldhaber found no case in which there is a statistically significant effect of private schools on math and reading test scores.

Although private school students have higher mean test scores than do public school students, the great majority of the mean differences between school sectors can be attributed to differences in the characteristics of students attending schools in those sectors rather than to differences in the effectiveness of these schools. Essentially, private schools attract students who are from better educated, wealthier families and who enter school with above average standardized test scores. These are students who would do well in both private and public schools.

These findings imply that, with a given set of schooling resources, there is no reason to believe that an average private school would do a better job of educating a group of students than an average public school would educate that same group of students. However, it is important to note that parents making these choices very often encounter situations where there are marked differences in the resources available in each school (Clotfelter, 1976).

To determine whether parents do, in fact, select schools based on educational quality, achievement differentials can be calculated that incorporate differences between the sectors in school resources, student bodies, and so on (see Goldhaber, 1997). These achievement differentials can be used to estimate a model of public–private school choice. The hypothesis is that parents are more likely to send their children to private school when estimated private school achievement is greater than the public school, and the probability grows as that gap increases. And conversely, they are more likely to send their children to public school when estimated public school achievement exceeds estimated private school achievement, and the probability grows as the gap increases. Also included in this model are controls for family background and for racial and income composition of the schools in each sector, all concerns of the liberal theorists and the critical pedagogues.

The results of the study show that parents, as expected, respond to these differences in estimated achievement. They are more likely to send their children to private schools as private sector achievement rises relative to public sector achievement. Thus, parents appear to be educated consumers in the sense that they select schools that benefit their children academically. This finding tends to support the proponents of school choice, like Friedman, Chubb and Moe, and Jencks, who argue that choice would create competition between schools based on school quality (see Hanushek, 1996).

CONSTITUTIONAL ISSUES

Another issue that is often brought forward by opponents of tuition vouchers is their alleged unconstitutionality. However, the most current court decisions seem to indicate that vouchers may well be found constitutional. The case that bears most relevance to the debate over vouchers is *Lemon v. Kurtzman*. In this case the Supreme Court set forth a test by which future cases regarding government aid to nonpublic schools would be judged in light of their compliance to the provisions of the Establishment Clause of the First Amendment to the U.S. Constitution. The Establishment Clause precludes the establishment of a religion by the state. The *Lemon* test is three-pronged, but a law need violate only one of the three to be found in violation of the Establishment Clause. The first step in the test asks whether the law has a secular purpose; the second asks if the laws' primary effect is to advance or inhibit religion, and the third step asks if there is excessive entanglement between the church and the State.

Milwaukee's school voucher program has been operating for nearly a decade. Initially, the city only allowed vouchers to be used to send students to nonreligious private schools. In 1995, however, the Wisconsin Legislature voted to include religious schools in the program. But the expansion was put on hold after it was challenged in court.

On June 10, 1998, the Wisconsin Supreme Court ruled that incorporating religious schools into the program did not violate either the state or the U.S. Constitution. Using the *Lemon* test, the court said the program's origin was driven largely by a "secular purpose"—to expand educational opportunities for poor children. Additionally, the court noted, any child attending a parochial school under the program could be excused from religious instruction if his or her parents requested such an exemption (see Palestini, 1999).

The American Civil Liberties Union, People for the American Way, and affiliates of the state's largest teachers' unions appealed the decision to the U.S. Supreme Court. Both supporters and opponents hoped a Supreme Court ruling would clarify what many view as a host of confusing and contradictory decisions on state support of religious schools.

Although the Supreme Court had never ruled on the constitutionality of vouchers, it had looked at other laws that helped parents with educational expenses. In 1973, for example, the court ruled in *Committee for Public Education and Religious Liberty v. Nyquist* that a New York state law granting parents reimbursements and tax credits for private school tuition was unconstitutional. The court said the law had the effect of subsidizing religious education because roughly three quarters of the parents receiving the reimbursements or credits sent their children to church-related schools.

But over the next two decades, the court handed down several apparently contradictory rulings, including *Mueller v. Allen* in 1983. In that case, the court held that an Ohio law offering a parental tax deduction for tuition was constitutional even though 93% of those claiming the deduction had children in the religious schools. In recent years, the Supreme Court has made a number of decisions that have broken down the wall separating church and state. For example, in 1998, *Agostino v. Felton* overturned *Aguilar v. Felton*, which allowed the state to provide auxiliary educational services inside the building of a religious school.

It was not surprising, therefore, that the Supreme Court's 8–1 decision not to review the Wisconsin case was widely interpreted as a victory for supporters of school choice. The Supreme Court has left intact "the most definitive court decision on vouchers to date, which solidly supports the constitutionality of school choice," said Michael McConnell (cited in Koch, 1999, p. 281), a law professor and constitutional scholar at the University of Utah. He said further that "the court's action clears the way for states to embark on further experiments with education choice." McConnell's words have proved to be prophetic in that several states have passed educational voucher bills based on a variety of theoretical modes since the Supreme Court's decision to leave the Milwaukee law intact. In fact, in *Zelman v. Simmons-Harris* (2003) the Supreme Court confirmed the constitutionality of tuition tax credits.

POLICY IMPLICATIONS AND CONCLUSIONS

What do all of these findings tell us? Both the direct and indirect evidence yields mixed results. There is no compelling empirical evidence that leads us to believe that school choice in any form will be a panacea for addressing the problems in our schools. On the other hand, to expect empirical evidence from such short-lived programs to be compelling is unreasonable. What we can reasonably conclude, however, is that school choice, where it has been implemented, has not had the catastrophic results that some opponents have predicted. In fact, there have been some very encouraging signs that, both public and nonpublic schools alike have been improved by the process. I know first hand that needed change takes place much more readily when the "Sword of Damocles" is hanging overhead. I can remember instances where teachers could not possibly find the time to give students more individual attention, or when suggested changes in teaching methodologies were mightily resisted. But when the same school was in danger of closing, all of a sudden, teachers found more time to devote to their at-risk students, and, all of a sudden, they began to adapt their teaching styles to the learning styles of their students.

In the September 15, 1999 issue of *Education Week*, a front-page headline read "Schools Hit By Vouchers Fight Back." The article speaks of changes that have occurred at the Spencer Bibbs Advanced Learning Academy in Florida as a result of competition from "voucher schools." Spencer Bibbs has incorporated a new dress code, as well as other more curricular and instructional changes. "The new dress code is a visible reminder of the less tangible changes staff members at Spencer Bibbs have made following their recent branding by the state as a failing school" (Schools hit, 1999). But Bibbs also became one of only two Florida schools where students were offered vouchers to attend another public or private school of their choice. So, as much as they loathe the new state policy, staff members say that they are determined to overcome the stigma and improve in the future. Interesting, isn't it, what creating a little "sense of urgency" in an institution can do. This incident at Spencer Bibbs Learning Academy leads me to believe that a carefully crafted school choice program could be an important component, albeit only one of several components, in a much needed and multifaceted plan for education reform.

What I have chosen to suggest is an approach that grows out of both the liberal and critical pedagogy traditions. The tension for me is that as an administrator, a market-driven approach is attractive, but as an educator, the liberal and critical pedagogy models are preferable. As an administrator, I would like to see the broadest possible population benefit from a reform like school choice. In this role I would call for an all-inclusive school choice plan driven by market forces, which would make vouchers available to all students. However, as an educator, I am concerned about pedagogy, equity, fairness, ethics, democracy, and serving the underserved. For these reasons, I much prefer to concentrate our limited resources where they can do the most good. Therefore, I am suggesting a modified or limited plan in which only the most needy would benefit.

I would suggest, then, that a school choice plan be structured according to the liberal and critical pedagogy traditions mentioned earlier. It should concern itself with cultural, societal and racial matters, and be as inclusive as possible. It should also concern itself with economic stratification, the distribution of power and the implied moral imperatives. Therefore, any proposed school choice plan should sound a caution regarding the equity consequences of choice. We cannot allow school choice plans to resegregate our schools, although we are currently far from truly integrating them.

Many educational researchers and practitioners suggest that our public schools are underfunded, and that if adequate funding were provided, many of the schools' alleged shortcomings would be eliminated. For example, if funds were available to support a class size limit of ten students, the at-risk and special learners could be given the attention that they need and achievement scores might significantly increase. I do not doubt the wisdom of this view. However, the chances of the American public making available the considerable amount of incremental revenue needed to accomplish the above are slim at best. Increased funding of public education does not seem to be something that will happen anytime soon. In the absence of any significant increase in funding for public schools, the school choice plan suggested here may be one of the few alternatives acceptable to most taxpayers to improve our schools. If it does not work, the argument for increased funding of public schools might become more palatable to the American taxpayer.

Studies also show that upper income families are clearly more likely to send their children to private schools (see Hawley, 1996). Thus, these families would be likely beneficiaries of any voucher plan like the one proposed in California. The $2,600 California voucher would probably have been too small to enable low-income families to afford high-quality private schools, but it would clearly have benefited those families whose children are already enrolled in the private sector or those upper income families for whom $2,600 would be enough incentive to tip the scale in favor of private schooling. In my view, this type of voucher plan would not meet the standards of the critical theorists. One way to counter the potential for greater economic stratification in a voucher plan would be to create a progressive voucher program. Progressiveness could be achieved by simply targeting the voucher to low-income families (as is the case in the Milwaukee plan) or by creating a sliding scale so that the size of the voucher would vary with income or with private school tuition.

Finally, let us discuss the implications that vouchers would have on the distribution of power in American education. Critical theorists concern themselves with the contradictions that occur in education. For example, the American belief in equality is in contradiction to the simultaneous promotion of practices that create inequality among various groups. Although its goal is equality, I concur with the critical theorists in believing that the current distribution of power in American education has lead to an inequality whereby our most needy students are being marginalized and underserved.

Currently, the power in American education is concentrated in the hands of politicians, boards of education, educational administrators, and unions. Although well meaning, certain of these decision makers have virtually excluded the parents and their children from any meaningful input into their process, and, as a result, have marginalized an entire strata of people. Among the most underrepresented groups in the education decision-making process are the parents of at-risk, minority, and low-income children. In my view, a finely crafted school choice program, limited to low-income families, would redistribute power by placing it in the hands of parents, giving them a chance to determine which educational setting best meets their children's needs.

A number of the current educational reform movements call for more parental involvement in school. No politically correct member of the public school establishment would speak against such a proposition. But the irony is that the very same advocates of parental involvement would likely be opponents of school choice. In my view, school choice is the epitome of parental involvement.

This book speaks to the need to examine American education through the dual lenses of inclusion and democracy. The democratic ideal implies that the individual, no matter his or her racial background, gender, or socioeconomic status, should be integrally involved in the shaping of public education. Applying the democratic ideal to education requires students and their parents to have a determining voice in where and how they are educated. For all of its significant contributions to American democracy, our current monolithic public school educational process has not attained the democratic ideal. The modified or mitigated school choice initiative in the critical pedagogy and liberal traditions that we are considering here would get us closer to the democratic ideal of affording more parents and their children the opportunity and ability to decide which type of school, public or nonpublic, best meets their educational needs. The economically advantaged already have that opportunity. The proposed school choice program would extend that opportunity to the poor and move us ever closer to full inclusiveness and the democratic ideal.

In conclusion, then, it is my hope that the contents of this chapter stimulates and enlightens the continuing discourse on this important issue.

Perhaps, school choice will make no substantial difference in how our young people progress academically. But at least the decision will be in the hands of those who have most at stake. As it is now, we are not very successful in educating low-income, at-risk students, but it is those other than their parents who are making the decisions that affect their lives. Our limited experience with school choice indicates that it can make a difference in the schooling of our most needy young people. So, why not give it a try?

REFERENCES

Berliner, D., & Biddle, B. (1995). *The manufactured crisis: Myths, fraud, and the attack on America's public schools.* Reading, MA: Addison-Wesley.

Buchanan, J., Tollison, R., & Tulloch, G. (1980). *Toward a theory of the rentseeking society.* College Station: Texas A&M University Press.

Capell, F.J. (1976). *A study of alternatives in American eduation, Vol VI: Student outcomes in Alum Rock, 1974-76* (R–2170/6 NIE). Santa Monica, CA: The Rand Corp.

Chubb, J., & Moe, T. (1991). America's public schools: Choice is a panacea. *The Brookings Review, 91,* 82.

Clotfelter, C. (1976). School desegregation, tipping, and private school enrollment. *Journal of Human Resources, 7,* 29.

Coleman, J., & Hoffer, T. (1987). *Public and private schools: The impact of communities.* New York: Basic Books.

Coleman, J., Hoffer, T., & Kilgore, S., (1982). *High, school achievement, catholic and public schools compared.* New York: Basic Books.

Colopy, K.W., & Tarr, H.C. (1994). *Minnesota's public school choice options.* Washington, DC: U.S. Department of Education/Policy Studies Associates.

Coons, J.E., & Sugarman, S.D. (1978). *Education by choice: The case for family control.* Berkeley: University of California Press.

Delany, T.J. (1995). Participation of rural students with disabilities and rural gifted students in open enrollment. *Rural Special Education Quarterly, 14,* 31.

Downs, A. (1951). *An economic theory of democracy.* New York: Harper Brothers.

Evans, W.N., & Schwab, R.M. (1996). Finishing high school and starting college, do catholic schools make a difference? *The Quarterly Journal of Economics, 110,* 941.

Fantini, M. (1973). *Public schools of choice.* New York: Simon & Schuster.

Friedman, M. (1955). The role of government in education. In R.A. Solo (Ed.), *Economics and the public interest* (pp. 127-134). New Brunswick, NJ: Rutgers University Press.

Friedman, M. (1962). *Capitalism and freedom.* Chicago: The University of Chicago Press.

Funkhouser, J.E., & Colopy, K.W. (1994). *Minnesota's open enrollment option: Impacts on school districts.* Washington, DC: U.S. Department of Education/Policy Studies Associates.

Gill, A., & Michael, R. (1992). Does drug use cover wages? *Journal of Political Economy, 82,* 863.

Gintis, H. (1995). The political economy of choice. *Teachers College Record, 96*(3), 492.

Gintis, H. (1989). *Unconventional wisdom: Essays in honor of John Kenneth Galbraith.* New York: Houghton-Mifflin.

Goldhaber, D. (1997). School choice as education reform. *Phi Delta Kappan, 79*(2), 143.

Goldhaber, D., & Brewer, D. (1997). Why don't schools and teachers seem to matter? *Journal of Human Resources, 32,* 505-523.

Goldhaber, D. (1997). Public and private high schools: Is school choice an answer to the productivity problem:, *Economics of Education Review, 15,* 96, 93.

Gollner, P. (1993, August 4). On the California ballot: Should the state help pay for private-school pupils? *New York Times,* p. B-9.

Hanushek, E. (1996). Conceptual and empirical issues in the estimation of educational production functions. *Journal of Human Resources, 14,* 351.

Hanushek, E. (1996). The economics of schooling: Production and efficiency in public schools. *Journal of Economic Literature, 24,* 1141-1178.

Hawley, W. D. (1996). The predictable consequences of school choice. *Education Week,* 56.

Hedges, L., Laine, R., & Greenwald, R. (1994). A meta-analysis of the effects of differential school inputs on student outcomes. *Educational Resources, 1,* 5-14.

Heneg, J.R. (1994). *Rethinking school choice: Limits of the market metaphor.* Princeton, NJ: Princeton University Press.

Hoxby, C.M., (1996). Are efficiency and equity in school finance substitutes or complements? *Journal of Economic Perspectives, 10,* 51.

Jencks, C. (1966). Is the public school obsolete? *The Public Interest, 2,* 18-27.

Koch, K. (1999). School vouchers. *The Congressional Quarterly Researcher, 9,* 281.

Kozol, J. (1991). *Salvage inequalities.* New York: Crown.

Lamdin, D., & Mintrom, M. (1997). School choice in theory and practice: Taking stock and looking ahead. *Education Economics, 5*(3), 211.

Lamdin, D.J. (1997). School choice in theory and practice: Taking stock and looking ahead. *Education Economics, 5*(3), 211.

Law, M.Y. (1994). The participation of students who are identified as gifted and talented in Minnesota's open enrollment option. *Journal for the Education of the Gifted, 17,* 276.

Levin, H.M., & Kelley, C. (1994). Can education do it alone? *Economics of Education Review, 13,* 97.

Lott, J.R., Jr., (1990). Why is education publicity provided? A critical survey. *Cato Journal, 7,* 475.

Lott, J.R., Jr., (1993). An explanation of public provision of schooling: The impotence of indoctrination. *Journal of Law and Economics, 33,*199.

Molnar, A. (1997). Why school reform is not enough to mend our civil society. *Contemporary Issues, 78*(2), 137.

Molnar, A., Farrell, W., Johnson, J., & Sapp, M. (1996). Research, politics, and the school choice agenda. *Phi Delta Kappan, 79*(2), 243.

Neal, D. (1997). The effects of catholic secondary education on educational achieve-ment. *Journal of Labor Economics, 15*, 98.

Odden, A., & Massy, W. (1992). *Education funding for schools and universities: Improving productivity and equity.* Los Angeles: University of Southern California.

Palestini, R.H. (1999). *Law and American education: A case brief approach.* Acton, MA: Copley.

Parry, T. (1997). Theory melts reality in the education voucher debate. *Education Economics, 5*(3), 307.

Sander, W., (1996). Catholic grade schools and academic achievement. *Journal of Human Resources, 31*, 540.

Schneider, M., Teske, P., Marscall, M., Mintrom, M., & Rooch, C. (1996). Institutional arrangements and the creation of social capital: The effects of pub-lic school choice, *American Political Sciences Review, 8*, 4.

Schools hit by vouchers fight back. (1999, September 15). *Education Week*, p. 56.

Tenbusch, J.P. (1993, April). *Parent choice behavior under Minnesota's open enroll-ment program.* Paper presented at the annual meeting of the American Eduation Research Association, Atlanta, GA.

Tenbusch, J.P., & Garet, N.S. (1993, April). *Organizational change at the local level under Minnesota's open enrollment program.* Paper presented at the annual meeting of the American Education Research Association, Atlanta, GA.

Toma, E.F. (1996). Public funding and private schooling across countries. *Journal of Law and Economics, 34*, 121.

Weiler, D.A. (1977). *Study of alternatives in American education: Summary and pol-icy implications (R–2170/7 NIE).* Santa Monica, CA: The Rand Corp.

Witte, J.F. (1992). Private school versus public school achievement; are there findings that should affect the educational choice debate? *Economics of Education Review, 11*, 371.

8

The Politics of School Safety

Going Beyond Reform to Inclusion

Donna C. Perone

Saint Joseph's University

Widespread concern about violence in U.S. schools has led to many antiviolence initiatives throughout the country. To date, there has been much discussion about which intervention strategies are most effective in making schools safe. However, all too often, the public's perception of school safety has been framed by sensational media coverage of violent school incidents, recent cases in point being the Littleton, Colorado and Jonesboro, Arkansas school shootings. In reaction to media saturation coverage of these violent events and the intense public pressure that followed, many school districts around the nation are rushing to install expensive (and in some cases extensive) security systems in schools. Increasingly, we are seeing methods traditionally used for crime control and prevention in the community being employed in public schools. Surveillance cameras, metal detectors, locker searches, strip searches, undercover police, and even SWAT teams are being included in many school safety plans. Some districts have even instituted mock anti-terrorist drills, reminiscent of the "duck and cover drills" of the Cold War era. Over the past several years there has also been an increase in the application of a zero tolerance policy not only regarding weapon and drug possession, but also concerning less serious school offenses. These are disturbing trends because they have the potential to erode the civil rights of students and the protective role of schools—two keystones of education in a democratic society. The problem with the "get tough" anti-crime approach is that it focuses on school safety through the restricted lens of crime prevention. This approach is based on the assumption that more security means safer schools. It relies on the interdiction and punishment of "offenders" as its primary strategy and school crime statistics as the primary measure of a "safe" school.

What is often left out of the public dialogue and the media coverage of this issue, however, is a broader definition of *safety*, a more critical one. If schools are to provide safe environments for all students and teachers, the definition of school safety must be more inclusive. The discussion about school safety must be expanded to encompass multiple perspectives on what makes schools safe, why, and for whom.

As educators, psychologists, and public health professionals have become more involved in research about school violence and safety, the dialogue has been reframed. Educators discuss school safety as part of the educational mission and as a function of "effective" schools (Purkey & Smith, 1983). Psychologists identify safety as a basic human need and a requirement for psychological health (American Psychological Association, 1996). Public health professionals are concerned about the epidemiology of violence. Clearly, school safety is more than a criminal justice issue. And, it is more than an educational, psychological and/or public health concern as well.

Providing safe schools can also be viewed as an issue of social justice and inclusion. Few would argue against the idea that in a democracy all children have the right to an education and that providing a safe educational environment is part of that right. But this is not reality for some students. It is a deplorable fact that many students, particularly students in inner-city schools, don't feel safe in school, nor on their way to and from school. Moreover, student perceptions of safety are profoundly influenced by culture, race, class, and gender differences. It is precisely these differences that are overlooked by the "one-size-fits-all" approach that is currently used to address safety concerns. An analysis of the influence of race/ethnicity, class and gender must inform the discussion about what makes schools "safe" and how safety is perceived and experienced by students from diverse groups. Recognition that school safety has different meanings for different constituencies will lead to a more inclusive definition of school safety, an increased understanding of differing student and teacher perceptions and behavior, and a broader, more equitable and culturally responsive repertoire of prevention and intervention strategies.

In this chapter, I discuss the politics of school safety. I explore multiple dimensions of "school safety," and examine the implications of a more inclusive definition of safety on educational policy. First, it is helpful to review a brief history.

HISTORICAL CONTEXT OF SCHOOL SAFETY

Public concern about school safety is not a new phenomenon. The level of attention it receives has waxed and waned, often influenced by socioeconomic political forces in the larger society, and by mass media coverage that shapes individual and social consciousness.

During the 19th century worldwide social and political upheaval, the growth of industrialism, changing economic conditions, and an increase in immigration led to support for the common school movement in the United States. Many children, from both rural and urban areas, did not attend school. Some, left to their own devices, turned to delinquent behavior. For public school reformers like Horace Mann, compulsory education was seen as a way to promote safety and the social order by teaching a common moral and political creed. Mann viewed schools as having a powerful role in socializing poor, minority and immigrant children, including those whose "noncompliant" behavior would previously have excluded them from school. By the end of the century, progressive educators like John Dewey had moved beyond the issue of whether or not all students should be required to attend school to an attempt to re-define the social role of schools in an urban industrial society.

In the 1950s, changes in postwar employment patterns, social demographics and urban migrations led to public concern about youth gangs in the community and a focus on delinquent, alienated or "antisocial" youth. Movies like *Blackboard Jungle* and *West Side Story* strongly dramatized the problem of alienated youth, racism and gangs and reflected an increasing fear of minorities and immigrants.

The 1950s also witnessed a growing Civil Rights Movement to end de-jure segregation in America. In the years following the 1954 Supreme Court decision of *Brown vs. Board of Education, Topeka*, school desegregation in the south became the focus of national attention. Once again, school safety was an issue. This time, the physical safety of African-American students became a pressing concern when the attempt to integrate schools in the South led to violent, racist attacks against young Black children seeking equal access to public education.

The 1960s and 1970s were times of continued social and political upheaval. Many students became politically engaged, calling for an end to the war in Vietnam, demonstrating for social justice, an end to racism and sexism, and challenging school authorities to make education "more relevant." De facto segregation of schools was also challenged through court-ordered bussing in northern cities. *School safety* became a code word for restoring "order" and "discipline" in schools. According to this point of view, students should get back down to the business of getting an education instead of protesting. The Safe School Study Report to Congress (National

Institute of Education, 1978), the first large-cale, national study on school violence and safety was in part an attempt to address student alienation and resistance demonstrated through involvement in the civil rights, anti-war, and student movements of the time.

The 1980s and 1990s were a time of retrenchment and a return to "normalcy" under the Reagan era. The end of the Cold War and the beginning of the so-called "new world order" reframed the national dialogue. *Back to basics, national standards,* and *school choice* were terms used to build support for a conservative educational agenda that emphasized curriculum standardization and school privatization.

Inner-city schools became increasingly segregated as middle-class White families continued to move out of the cities, followed by middle-class African-American families. This led to the neglect and abandonment of urban neighborhoods and inner-city public schools. De facto school segregation increased as courts began to pull back from their attempts to integrate (Orfield & Eaton, 1996). School funding to inner-city schools began to decline in comparison to suburban schools. In his book, *Savage Inequalities,* Kozol (1991) painted a poignant picture of the disparity of public education funding, school resources and the quality of education between urban and suburban schools, and the devastating effect this disparity has on inner-city students' and teachers' attitude, expectations, and academic experience.

The late 1980s and the decade of the 1990s witnessed strengthening economic indicators, a booming economy, and an unprecedented rise in the stock market. This increased prosperity did not "trickle down," as promised, to the poor. Once again, the disparity between rich and poor began to grow. Of school-aged children, 25% lived below the poverty level (Children's Defense Fund, 1999). Along with the increase in poverty, joblessness, and hopelessness in inner-city minority neighborhoods, there was a proliferation of drugs and guns among urban youth and a rise in youth-based community violence, particularly homicides involving guns. This led juvenile justice professionals to call youth violence an "epidemic," public health professionals to declare it a "public health" problem, and psychologists to link youth violence to developmental and psychological "harm."

A renewed call for school safety echoed throughout the executive and legislative branches of government. In 1990, the National Education Goals Panel was commissioned by George Bush. Influenced by the conservative political agenda of the Reagan/Bush era and the *Nation At Risk* (National Commission on Excellence in Education, 1983) report, its mandate was to study public education in the United States and to make recommendations for improving the education and training of American youth in the face of increasing global economic competition and technological advances. Goal Seven of the Goals 2000 Educate America Act (National Education goals Panel, 1990) focused on the importance of "safe and disciplined" schools. In

1994, Congress passed the Safe Schools Act that authorized funding and technical assistance to school districts in order to develop safe school plans; and the Gun Free Schools Act that directed states to implement a zero tolerance policy on weapons at school.

One of the common elements linking the events just outlined is the way in which school safety has been defined. Safe schools were assumed to be "orderly" schools where the students were "well-disciplined" and where there was an absence of school crime or violence. This is often the underlying assumption of many school boards and politicians as they call for "locking down" schools in order to make them safe. Because such actions are highly visible, they may appear to be effective. But, there is little systematic evidence to support the notion that a reliance on increased police presence or tightening school security will lead to school safety. The prison metaphor (lock down) is not coincidental. The "law and order" approach to school safety is the cornerstone of a conservative political agenda that is more concerned with punishment than proactive change and reform. The prison metaphor also serves to highlight the fallacy of this approach. Presumably, there is nowhere more "secure" than a prison; yet increased security and "lock downs" do not necessarily make prisons safe. Why, then, should we assume this approach would necessarily make schools safe? Installing metal detectors in schools has also been likened to installing metal detectors in airports. An equally faulty assumption underlines the comparison of school security to airport security. Airports are anonymous places through which many unfamiliar people pass on their way to somewhere else. There is no presumed connection to one another, no expectation of meaningful relationship. Hopefully, we will not yield to those who seek to apply these models to schools!

SCHOOLS AS COMMUNITIES

Schools are not anonymous public spaces, but mini communities where students and teachers, administrators, and parents have daily contact and establish meaningful ties. In fact, the public expectation is that schools in a democratic society should be protective places that provide children safe, supportive, and inclusive environments, places where both intellectual and psychosocial development is promoted and realized. This expectation has its roots in the philosophy of John Dewey who espoused the idea of schools as communities in the late 19th and early 20th centuries. In an early statement of his educational philosophy, Dewey (1897) declared "Much of present education fails because it neglects the fundamental principle of the school as a form of community life." Concerned with the negative effects of urbanization and industrialization, and attempting to understand the dynamic, reciprocal relationship of the individual to the community, Dewey linked the educational process with the psychological and sociological dimensions of a child's experience. He envisioned a multidimensional model where the child grows not in isolation, but in interaction with the social environment. Dewey believed schools should foster a spirit of "cooperation and community" leading to the development of critical thinking skills necessary for participation in a democratic society. Unfortunately, this expectation has been more of an ideal than a reality for many public schools. And, Dewey's vision has been especially, and cruelly one might add, elusive for inner-city, and rural, poor and minority students throughout the country. One hundred years later, Dewey's vision of schools as protective and fertile environments for the healthy development of children has not been realized for many school-aged children, particularly not for poor and minority children.

SCHOOL SAFETY:
MULTIPLE PERCEPTIONS, MULTIPLE MEANINGS

National Studies of middle and high school students released by the U.S. Departments of Education and Justice (1998) have found that, despite a decrease in some school crime indicators such as fighting and weapon carrying, there was no change in the number of students reporting being afraid in school. Clearly, an analysis of school crime statistics, although necessary, is not sufficient to understand student perceptions of safety. What other factors are students responding to?

A critical analysis of school safety goes beyond the mere tallying of incidents of violence and seeks to incorporate multiple perspectives on safety. Different constituencies have different perceptions about what makes schools safe. We witness daily the power of the media to shape public perceptions about schools and school safety. Students and teachers often differ in their perceptions. Differences in perceptions are also influenced by age, race, class, and gender differences. We hear about the link between crime and violence or psychological disturbance and violent behavior. However, we don't often hear how violent behavior in many inner-city urban schools is rooted in fear, injustice, poverty, racism, sexism, de-facto segregation, disenfranchised parents, racially isolated communities and lowered student and teacher expectations. Just as there are different perceptions about what makes a school safe, there are different theoretical approaches to analyzing school safety and to implementing intervention policy. The three approaches I discuss in this chapter I call the *conservative*, *liberal*, and *critical* theoretical approaches. These approaches are driven by different sociopolitical views of the role of schools in society and the relationship of power within schools. In the following section, I discuss these different theoretical paradigms, their goals and their impact on educational policy regarding school safety, and why we need to go "beyond reform to inclusion" in our efforts to make schools safe.

THEORETICAL APPROACHES TO SCHOOL SAFETY

The Conservative Approach

The conservative approach is concerned with the goal of maintaining social control in schools through the use of discipline, and force if necessary. The conservative theoretical approach has had a great influence on educational policy and programs. For many years, school violence and safety have been seen more as a criminal justice issue, not an educational issue. The focus is on school violence, not school safety. In fact, school safety is defined as the lack of school violence. This approach has led to a reliance on analysis of school crime data. Statistics such as number of students suspended, expelled, or arrested for criminal acts are used as a measure of effectiveness of violence intervention efforts. Solutions are based on increased discipline, insistence on compliance with rules, stricter enforcement of consequences, zero tolerance, installation of security measures such as metal detectors and video cameras, more police presence, and changes in the building plant.

The conservative approach is based on the belief that the role of schools is to maintain the "status quo." In other words, the purpose of schooling is to reinforce the existing social and political order. Students and teachers are expected to assume their traditional, hierarchical roles within the school's social structure. Effects of this "top–down" approach have been an increased tendency of school officials to adopt "get tough" policies to keep order and to assert their power and authority; a reliance on suspension as the disciplinary method of choice; and expulsion of students who are "chronic offenders." Some conservatives have even called for an end to compulsory education (Toby, 1983) so that schools, they say, can exclude those students who, by their misbehavior, show they don't really want to be in school anyway. Conservative school officials are also more apt to subscribe to a zero tolerance policy, treating student misbehavior as a criminal offense to be handled by the police and courts, rather than by school personnel; and/or by making changes to the school environment.

These get tough measures are often a response to a pervasive public concern about discipline and violence in schools, fueled by sensational media coverage and political rhetoric. Increased security measures may seem effective because they are highly visible. However, they may have the opposite effect, and ironically, may contribute to increased student resentment, alienation and misbehavior.

During the Reagan/Bush administrations, tougher crime bills led to the building of more prisons, and policies based on punitiveness rather than rehabilitation. Conservatives have a similar approach to schools. They talk about "anarchy" in public schools and the need to "take back" our schools. Their agenda for school reform focuses on the back-to-basics movement. The notion of back-to-basics goes hand in hand with zero tolerance in that both rely on power of authority and the reliance on fixed standards rather than consensus of ideas or concern for individual differences. Basic skills programs have been initiated as a "reform" by state governments around the country, grounded in the notions of a "functional" curriculum, "outcomes-based" evaluation, and "minimum competency" testing. An emphasis on standardized testing is prominent. Conservatives call for a standardized curricula, and have little tolerance for diversity and multiculturalism. Deficit theories of culture and education frame the conservative response to urban school problems (Nieto, 2000). Poor performance or misbehavior is presumed to be an inherent characteristic of inner-city minority students, rather than a function of the interaction of factors in the school environment. A "blame the victim" (Ryan, 1972) attitude is at the heart of these responses, and, in many cases, a racist, or Social Darwinist view that believes certain groups are inherently "superior" than others.

The Liberal Approach

The liberal theoretical position takes a less punitive, more humanistic approach to discipline and school violence reduction. The goal of liberal school safety efforts is prevention more than intervention. Liberal efforts are aimed at reform of the environment or current school practices in order to maximize student achievement and development.

Much of the focus nowadays is on the individual student, with a view toward identification of "at-risk," or "potentially violent" students in order to intervene with counseling or social services. The problem with this strategy is there are no reliable and valid ways to identify the "potential" for violence. Here, the line between conservative and liberal political agendas gets very blurry. Proponents of programs designed to early identify and target violent youth argue that the purpose is to help, not harm, by providing the needed services and agency coordination required to monitor and rehabilitate delinquent or pre-delinquent youth. This argument sounds good, but can have undesirable consequences. For example, profiles and checklists used currently to early identify "potentially violent" students may over-identify, or misidentify students. This leads to lowered expectations for those students in school and in the community, and the risk of creating a self-fulfilling prophecy (Rosenthal & Jacobson, 1968). This, together with the effects of race and class biases on lowered expectations for poor and minority youth in general, will have an even greater devastating effect on the academic and social well being of inner-city students.

During the latter part of the 1990s, a more proactive, student-centered approach to violence reduction was the popularization of conflict resolution and peer mediation programs among school districts. The objective of these programs is to provide students with the knowledge and skills to resolve disputes without resorting to violence. Peer tutoring, cooperative learning, and mentoring techniques are also used to provide at-risk students with individual attention, positive peer models, and adult support. Within this model, teachers are encouraged to use antiviolence curricula and social skills training as a way to improve peer relations, social problem solving, and communication skills. Counseling and interagency intervention programs are also implemented to provide a network of resources available to students and their families in school. Recognizing that schools cannot solve the problems of at-risk youth in isolation, school districts are beginning to form collaboratives with other agencies in their community in order to provide a more comprehensive approach to intervention and prevention (Hawkins & Catalano, 1994). In this model, the school building frequently becomes the center of service delivery, facilitating interagency coordination, and increased access to services for families.

The school reform movement of the 1980s, with its emphasis on school effectiveness and teacher effectiveness, has had an important influence on liberal strategies to promote safe schools through making changes at the system level. Violence reduction efforts have targeted changes in the school's organizational and management structure, looking to develop strong leadership in schools (not the bat-wielding type of principal typified by Joe Clark in Paterson, New Jersey). Some school districts have implemented shared decision making, encouraging the participation of all stakeholders through school-based management in order to make education more responsive to students and their families. Within this model, student participation is talked about in order to improve student engagement, however, few vehicles for meaningful participation are actually available to students in most schools. Middle and high school students often complain about not having a voice in what goes on in schools and feel that their input on educational questions is not taken seriously.

Educators and policymakers have looked to school climate theory as a way to understand how various factors within the school environment impact on student behavior, and for keys to a more comprehensive violence prevention and intervention strategy. A systems-level, or ecological perspective (Bronfenbrenner, 1979) that looks at the interaction of the individual with the school and community, is the basis for school climate improvement efforts. Implicit in this perspective is the understanding that although individual characteristics are critical in explaining behavior, the social context to which an individual is exposed makes a significant contribution. Dividing large schools into smaller units (or schools within schools), for example, has been a found to improve communication between staff and administration, teacher–student relations, academic achievement, and student behavior.

Liberal policy is ambivalent about multiculturalism. Multicultural education is talked about, but usually superficially implemented. Curriculum content and values taught in schools are presumed to be "universal," but, in fact, reflect a White, middle-class experience and perspective. There is also a presumption that hard work will lead to social mobility, and that, ultimately, the system works for most people. Of course, the liberal presumption of equality in a democracy is questionable. Clearly, everyone does not have an "equal" voice.

The Critical Theoretical Approach

Conservative and liberal theorists agree that the purpose of schooling is to preserve the social order either by reproducing, or reforming, the status quo. Critical theorists on the other hand, view the purpose of schooling as *transformative*. For critical theorists, knowledge is neither neutral nor apolitical (Freire, 1985). Critical theory assumes that schools are places where power struggles between dominant and subordinate groups take place. Critical theorists attempt to reveal the ways in which dominant ideology is translated into school practices and the ways in which "human agency" counteracts the impact of that ideology (Bennett de Marrais & LeCompte, 1999). Critical theorists look at how schools reproduce inequality both structurally and functionally. Critical theorists point to the contradiction between an educational system that on the one hand preaches equal opportunity through values such as hard work, self-discipline, motivation, and responsibility, and on the other hand perpetuates inequality within social, cultural, and economic relations (Giroux, 1988). A critical analysis of school safety looks at the multiple social and cultural relationships that exist in schools among students, teachers, and administrators and asks: "What are the structural and cultural aspects of schools that reinforce a school system that alienates, oppresses, and subordinates teachers and students leading to more violence, or a lack of safety?" The possibility of hope and change for public education lies in a serious dialogue around these very questions.

Critical theory analyzes multiple perspectives on school safety and on multiple levels. Different perspectives based on experiences due to race, class, and gender lead to different definitions of what makes an individual feel safe. For example, critical theorists look at the influence of race/ethnicity on student and teacher perceptions of safety. Inner-city minority students often live in segregated neighborhoods. Poverty, crime, and depriva-tion plague many of these neighborhoods. Often, students are fearful in their neighborhoods. Daily feelings of fear may contribute to hypervigilance in school. It is not uncommon to hear some students say they bring knives, box cutters, guns, or other weapons to school to "protect" themselves and to feel "safe." Many students report staying home from school out of fear of being bullied or attacked by other classmates. Students from other countries who speak little English may feel unsafe and insecure in unfamiliar urban school environments and opt to stay home, or drop out. It is this feeling of fear and alienation that we must address in order to make schools safe for children. School safety efforts that focus only on weapon control are doomed to failure because they miss this point entirely.

Issues of race, class, and gender influence the relationship between stu-dents and teachers as well. For example, often, in inner-city schools, teachers are mostly White, middle class, and live in relatively affluent suburbs, where-as the students they teach are mostly Black, Latino, or Asian, poor, and live in relative deprivation (Anyon, 1997). How does this gulf between teacher and student experience influence the way teachers and students interact in schools? How do these differences impact on teacher and student percep-tions of school safety, what it means to be "safe." How do these differences effect teacher expectations? Frequently, these differences are not addressed, or swept under the rug, as if they did not matter, or were not relevant to the educational process. But these differences do, in fact, matter. They influence perceptions, expectations and behavior. Although most teachers claim to have high expectations of their students, all too often minority students are not expected to achieve as much as White students. Low expectations can have a devastating effect on student performance and behavior. Moreover, students will not feel "safe" with teachers who do not believe in their ability and who do not challenge them educationally in worthwhile ways. Many teachers will not "go the extra mile" for students whom they perceive have little chance to succeed. When students do not have satisfying relationships within schools, when they feel devalued, put down, rejected, or bullied, or when they do not believe they have a voice within a larger school communi-ty, they often become anxious, resentful and fearful, thereby increasing their alienation and reducing their motivation to learn and achieve.

Critical theorists question the relationship between institutional inter-ests, power, and what gets included in, or excluded from, the school curricu-lum. Critical theory looks at the impact of institutional racism on school safety. When inner-city schools are neglected, receive less funding than sub-urban schools, are not connected to the communities in which they are located, and serve as "holding places" for students, there is a vicious contra-diction between the stated goals of education and the reality for urban youth.

CONCLUSION

Perceptions of school safety, climate, and violence often depend on political perspective; be it conservative, liberal or critical theoretical. The policies proposed by each follow an internal logic that unfolds from the point of view of the policymaker.

The conservative and liberal approaches, although they may appear to be "objective," run contrary to the goal of inclusion because the perspectives of minorities, women, and others are not accorded equal weight in the public debate. This is because objectivity is defined from the point of view of the status quo.

Frequently, the public, through the mass media, is given an "either–or" choice between the liberal and conservative viewpoints. Other points of view are excluded. Conservatives are increasingly using prisons as their model for safe schools. Liberals are looking to models that purport to identify characteristics which they believe are predictive of potential for violence in individuals. This viewpoint contains an inherent danger of "profiling" individuals.

Critical theorists offer an alternative to these two viewpoints by emphasizing the need for inclusion. Making schools "safe" requires strategies that go beyond traditional notions of safety as merely the absence of violence or threat to personal security. It requires strategies that go beyond piecemeal school reform, or implementing the intervention program de jour. Making schools safe requires a more critical, inclusive and transformational approach. Looking at safety critically, from multiple perspectives, and on multiple levels, provides a more complete understanding of the interrelation of socioeconomic, race, gender, and culture factors in schools and how these factors shape student behavior, perceptions and social relations within schools. Ultimately, it is the quality of school social relations and the feeling of community that sets the stage for a safe and nurturing educational environment. We must make it our business to ensure that all children attend such schools.

REFERENCES

American Psychological Association. (1996). *Violence & youth: Psychology's response. Volume 1: Summary report of the American Psychological Association Commission on Violence and Youth.* Washington, DC: Author.

Anyon, J. (1997). *Ghetto schooling: A political economy of urban educational reform.* New York: Teachers' College Press.

Bennett de Marrais, K., & LeCompte, M.D. (1999). *The ways schools work: A sociological analysis of education* (3rd ed.). Boston: Allyn & Bacon.

Bronfenbrenner, U. (1979). *The ecology of human development: Experiments by nature and design.* Cambridge, MA: Harvard University Press.

Brown v. Board of Education of Topeka, KS, 349 U.S. 294 (1955).

Children's Defense Fund. (1999). *The state of America's children.* Washington, DC: Author.

Dewey, J. (1897). My pedagogic creed. *The School Journal, 54*(3), 77-80.

Freire, P. (1985). *The politics of education: Culture, power and liberation.* South Hadley, MA: Bergin & Garvey.

Giroux, H. (1988). *Schooling and the struggle for public life: Critical pedagogy in the modern age.* Minneapolis: University of Minnesota Press.

Hawkins, D., & Catalano, R. (1994). *Communities that care: Risk focused prevention using the social development strategy.* Seattle, WA: Social Development Research Group.

Kozol, J. (1991). *Savage inequalities.* New York: Crown.

National Commission on Excellence in Education. (1983). *A nation at risk: The imperative for educational reform.* Washington, DC: Author.

National Education Goals Panel. (1990). *Building a nation of learners.* Washington, DC: Author.

National Institute of Education. (1978). *Violent schools—safe schools: The safe school study report to Congress.* Washington DC: Department of Health, Education & Welfare, U.S. Government Printing Office.

Nieto, S. (2000). *Affirming diversity: The sociopolitical context of multicultural education.* New York: Longman.

Orfield, G., & Eaton, S.E. (1996). *Dismantling desegregation: The quiet reversal of Brown v. Board of Education.* New York: The New Press.

Purkey, S., & Smith, M. (1983). Effective schools: A review. *Elementary School Journal, 83*(4), 427-452.

Rosenthal, R., & Jacobson, L. (1968). *Pygmalion in the classroom.* New York: Holt, Rinehart & Winston.

Ryan, W. (1972). *Blaming the victim.* New York: Vintage Books.

Toby, J. (1983). Violence in school. In M. Tonry & N. Morris (Eds.), *Crime and justice: An annual review of research, 4.* Chicago: University of Chicago Press.

U.S. Departments of Education and Justice. (1998). *Annual report on school safety.* Washington, DC: NCES 98-251/NCJ-172215.

U.S. Senate. (1994). *Safe School Act of 1994.* (S. 1125, 103rd Congress).

Author Index

A

Alton-Lee, A., 26, 31, *41*

American Association for the Advancement of Science, 112, 115, 116, 117, 121, 122, 123, 126, 127, *134*

American Psychological Association. 164, *174*

Anyon, J., 2, *6*, 173, *174*

Apple, M., 14, *21*

Applegate, M.D., 44, *64*

Apt-Perkins, D., 70, 83, *86*

Aronoff, M., 26(*n*1), *41*

Ayers, W., 19, *21*

B

Banks, J., 68, 69, 70, 72, 75, *86*

Beane, J., 10, 15, 17, 18, *21*

Bennett de Marrais, L., 172, *174*

B

Berger, R., 32, *41*

Berliner, D., 144, 153, *159*

Beyer, L., 18, *21*

Biddle, B., 144, 153, *159*

Brady, J., 11, 14, *21*, 47, *65*

Brewer, D., 145, 153, *160*

Britzman, D., 18, *21*, 69, *86*

Bronfenbrenner, U., 171, *175*

Brown v. Board of Education of Topeka, KS, 165, *175*

Buchanan, J., 142, *159*

Buchmann, M., 69, *86*

C

Capell, F.J., 147, *159*

Carifio, J., 47, 57, 58, 59, 60, 61, 62, 63, *64*

Catalano, R., 171, *175*

Chilcoat, G., 35, 36, *41*

Subject Index

Printed in the United States
50360LVS00003B/232-237

9 781572 734647